FOR ORGANS, PIANOS & ELECTRONIC KEYBOARDS

E-Z PLAY TODAY

97

Elvis Presley
SONGS OF INSPIRATION

T0040925

ISBN 978-0-7935-3272-8

HAL•LEONARD®
CORPORATION
7777 W. BLUEMOUND RD. P.O. BOX 13819 MILWAUKEE, WI 53213

Elvis Presley
SONGS OF INSPIRATION

Rockabilly, rhythm-and-blues, pop, country, and gospel music. Elvis sang it all with such feeling, such integrity, such artistry and soul. He did more than entertain. He seemed somehow to reach deep inside himself and, through his recordings and concert performances, communicate a feeling of closeness, warmth, and familiarity with his audience. They all felt as though they knew him and that he knew them. He revealed so much of himself to them through his music, maybe more than he realized. He was deeply spiritual, and there was a particular closeness between him and his audience when he sang gospel.

Elvis listened to, sang, and absorbed musical influences of all kinds in his youth. Gospel was a tremendous part of that. He grew up in the Assembly of God Church, and the richness and power of the music he heard and sang there with his family had a profound effect on him as a person and on the unique musical sound and feel he would develop as a professional singer. As a teenager in Memphis, he regularly attended the all-night gospel sings. This kid with the sideburns and flashy clothes became a regular fixture backstage, meeting and talking with the singers he admired so much.

One of those performers was the now-legendary bass singer J.D. Sumner. J.D. and the others would always expect to see Elvis whenever they were in town. One night, the kid wasn't there, and when they saw him the next time they played Memphis, J.D. asked why he hadn't attended. Elvis confided that he simply had not had the money for a ticket. J.D. made sure Elvis got in free from then on as his special guest. Years later, J.D. and a group he then led, the Stamps, backed Elvis the superstar on record and in concerts in the 1970's.

"We do two shows a night for five weeks. A lotta times we'll go upstairs and sing until daylight—gospel songs. We grew up with it...it more or less puts your mind at ease.
It does mine."

Elvis Presley
1972

When Elvis said this he was talking about how he and the musicians in his show would play those month-long Vegas engagements, and, with the energy still surging within them from the concerts just performed, they would gather in Elvis' suite at the Vegas Hilton and do the last thing you'd expect a bunch of singers to do after pouring their all into two shows a night—they'd sing some more! An enormous part of all these after-show jam sessions was gospel music. It was also a big part of the casual get-togethers around the piano back home at Graceland.

The gospel feel in Elvis' music also ran through his pop, country, and even rock-and-roll recordings and performances. From 1956 through most of the sixties, Elvis' backing vocal group was the Jordanaires. In the concert years of the 1970's, Elvis was backed on stage and on record by The Imperials and then by J.D. Sumner and the Stamps Quartet. The sound and feel of black female gospel was provided by the Sweet Inspirations. It is also interesting to note that out of the fourteen Grammy nominations received by the man known as the "king of rock and roll", his three Grammy wins were all for gospel. He won Best Sacred Performance for his recording of "How Great Thou Art" in 1967, Best Inspirational Performance for his album "He Touched Me" in 1972, and Best Inspirational Performance in 1974 for a live concert version of "How Great Thou Art". As much as gospel music meant to him, he surely must have been very pleased to have this facet of his career honored in such a way.

Here, we present "Elvis Presley—Songs Of Inspiration", a selection of material he recorded on his various gospel albums for RCA Records, music that was close to his heart and a big part of his life.

Amazing Grace

Registration 2
Rhythm: Waltz

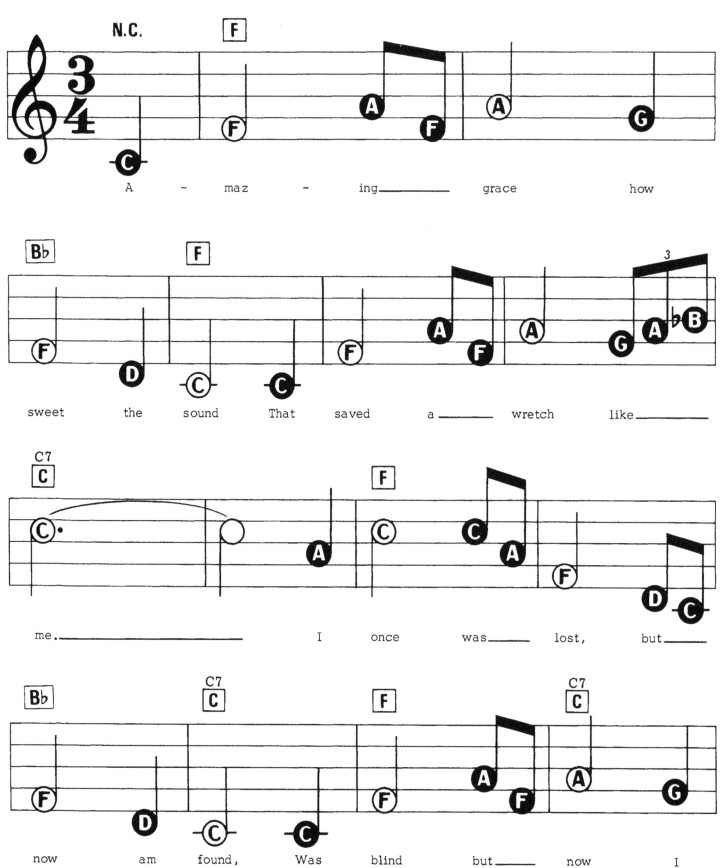

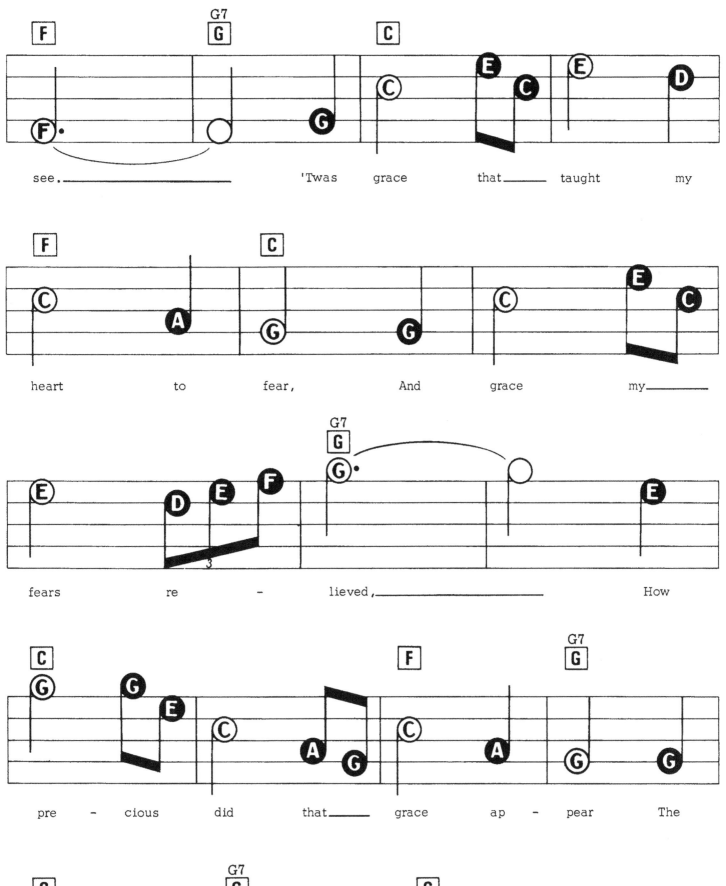

see._____ 'Twas grace that____ taught my

heart to fear, And grace my_____

fears re - lieved,_____ How

pre - cious did that____ grace ap - pear The

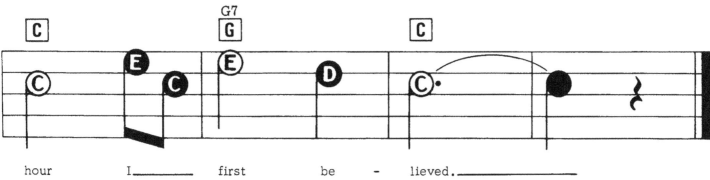

hour I____ first be - lieved._____

Bosom Of Abraham

Registration 4
Rhythm: Rock or Pops

Words and Music by William Johnson,
George McFadden and Ted Brooks

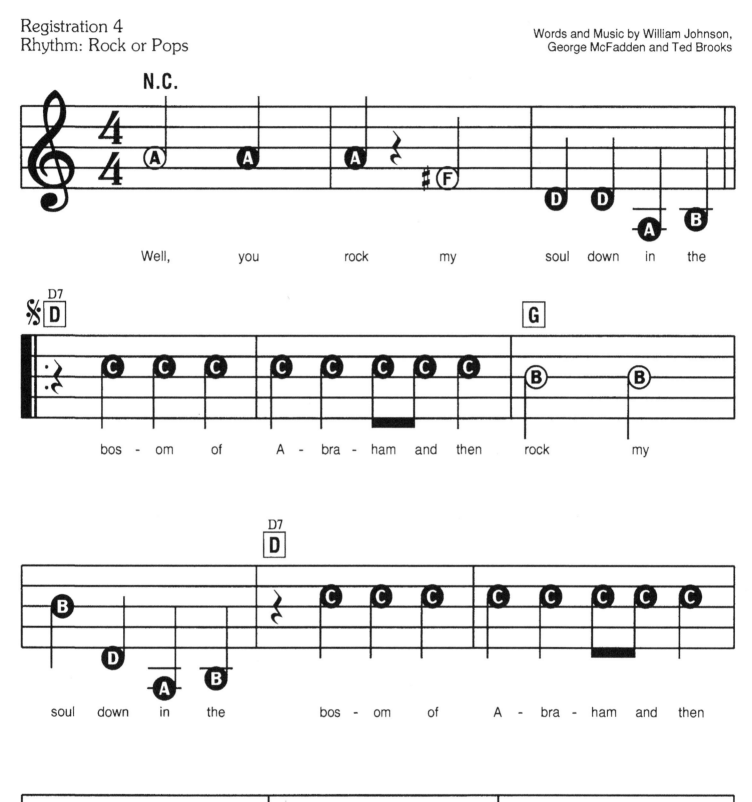

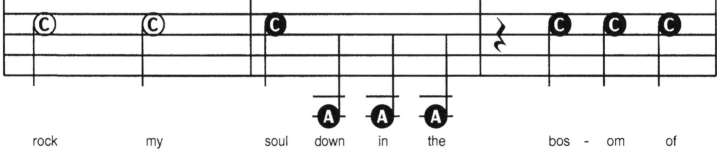

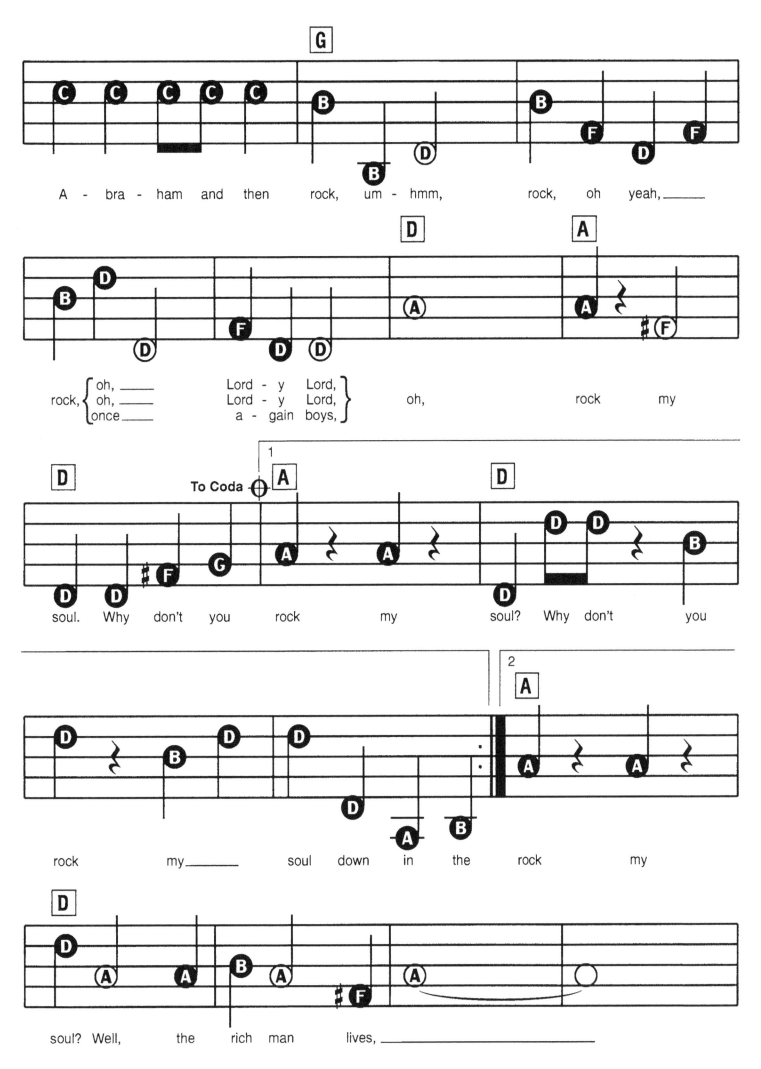

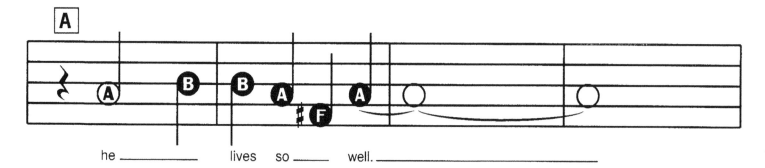

he _____ lives so _____ well. _____

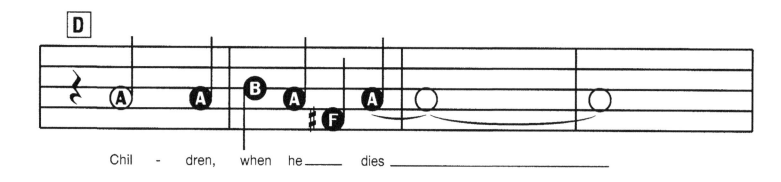

Chil - dren, when he_____ dies _____

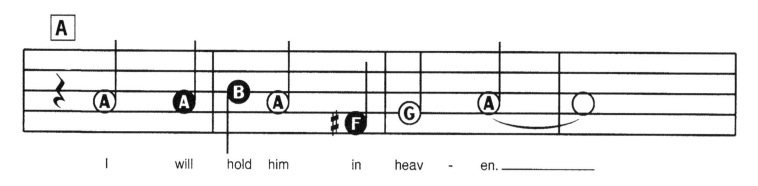

I will hold him in heav - en. _____

D.S. al Coda
(Return to %
Play to ⊕ and
Skip to Coda)

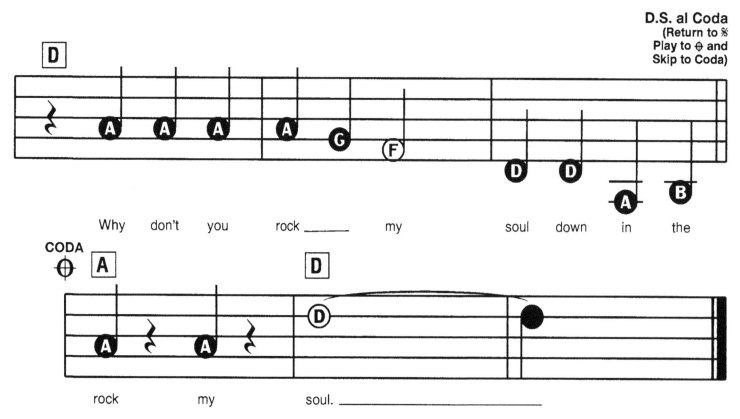

Why don't you rock _____ my soul down in the

rock my soul. _____

By And By

Registration 9
Rhythm: March or Rock

Adapted and Arranged by
Elvis Presley

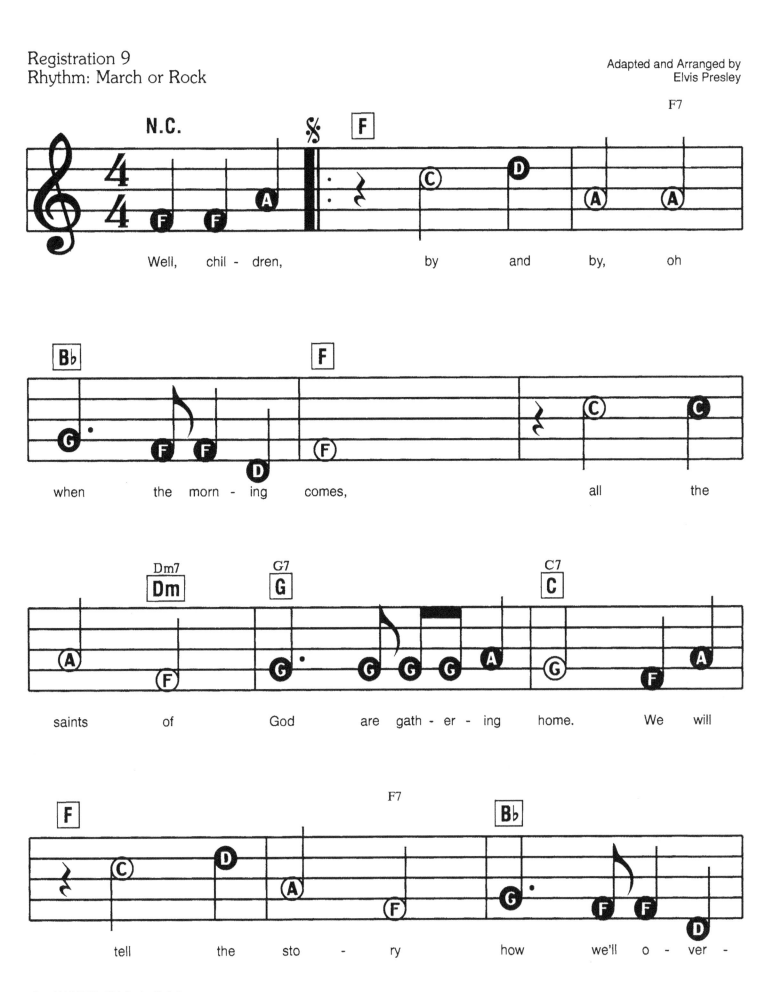

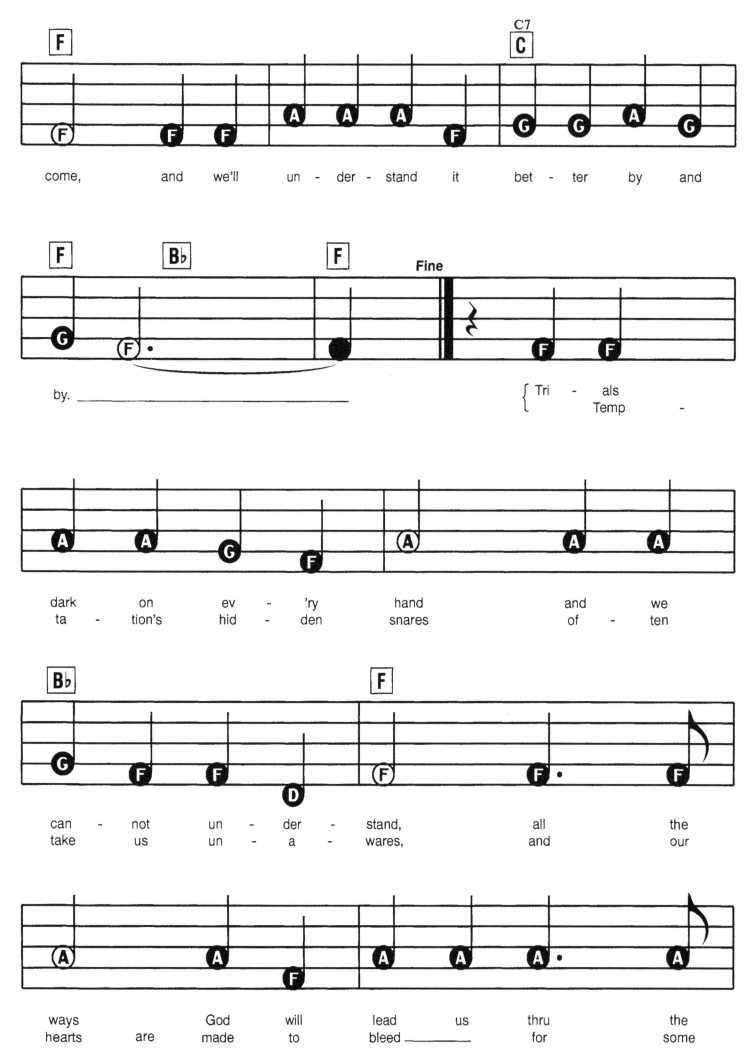

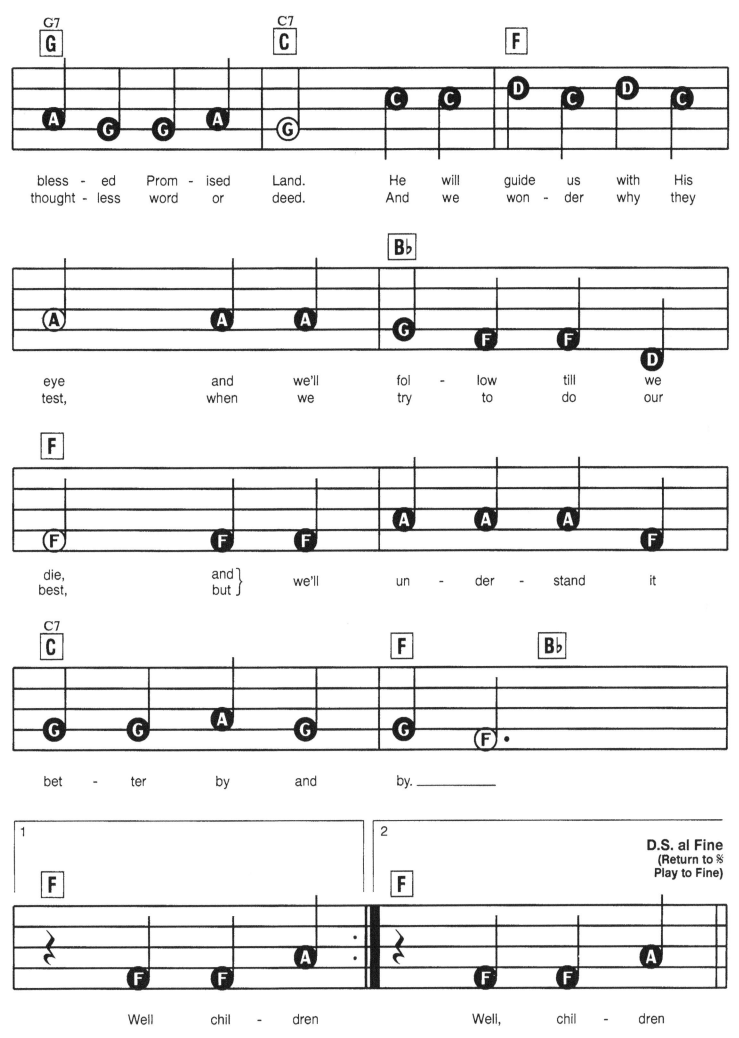

bless - ed Prom - ised Land. He will guide us with His
thought - less word or deed. And we won - der why they

eye and we'll fol - low till we
test, when we try to do our

die, and } we'll un - der - stand it
best, but }

bet - ter by and by. _____

1

F

Well chil - dren

2

D.S. al Fine
(Return to %
Play to Fine)

F

Well, chil - dren

Crying In The Chapel

Registration 2
Rhythm: Swing

Words and Music by
Artie Glenn

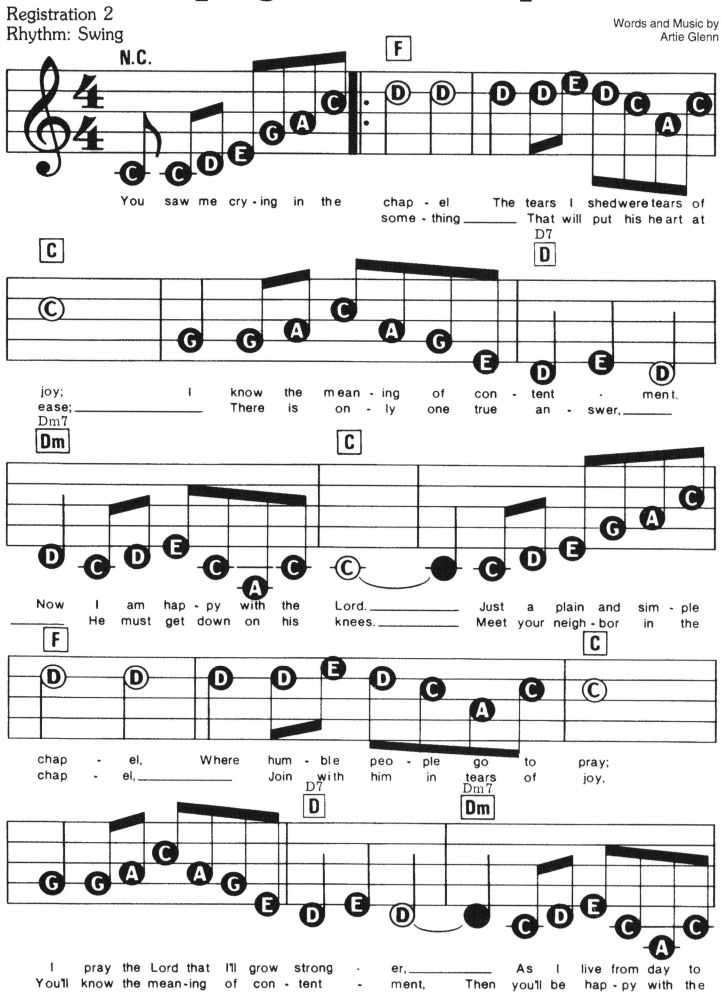

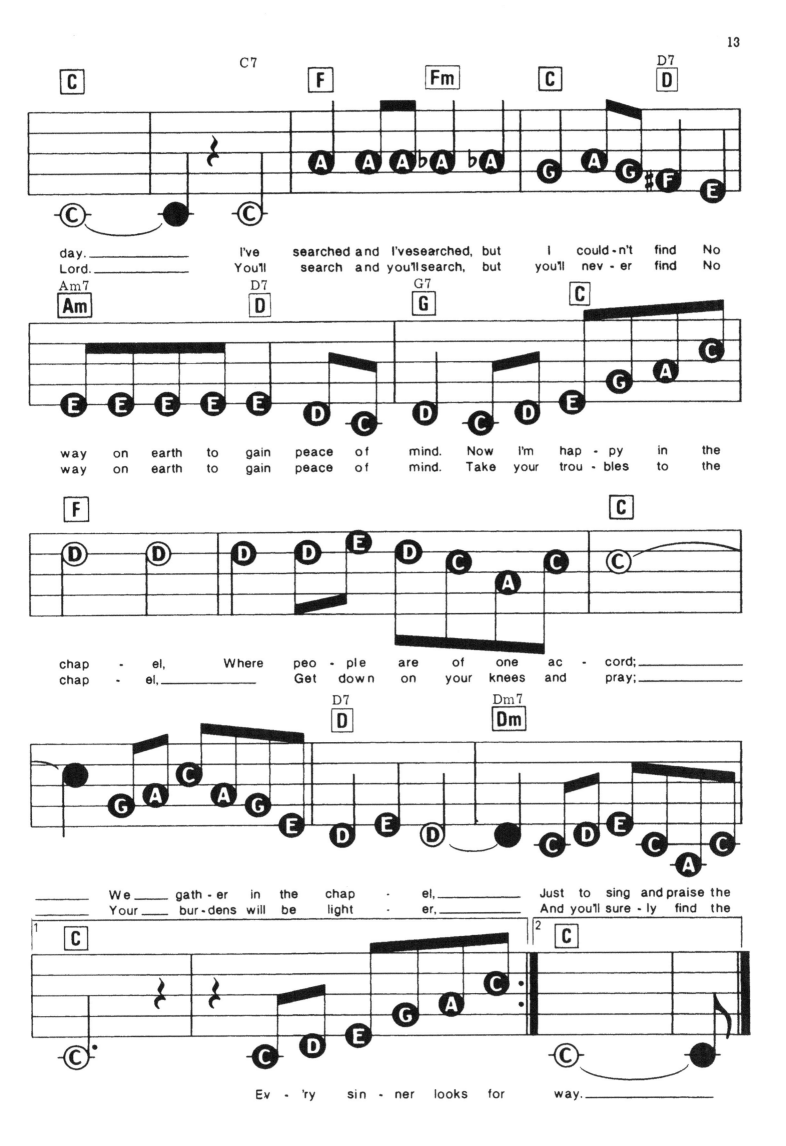

An Evening Prayer

Registration 4
Rhythm: 8 Beat or Rock

By C.M. Battersby
and Chas. H. Gabriel

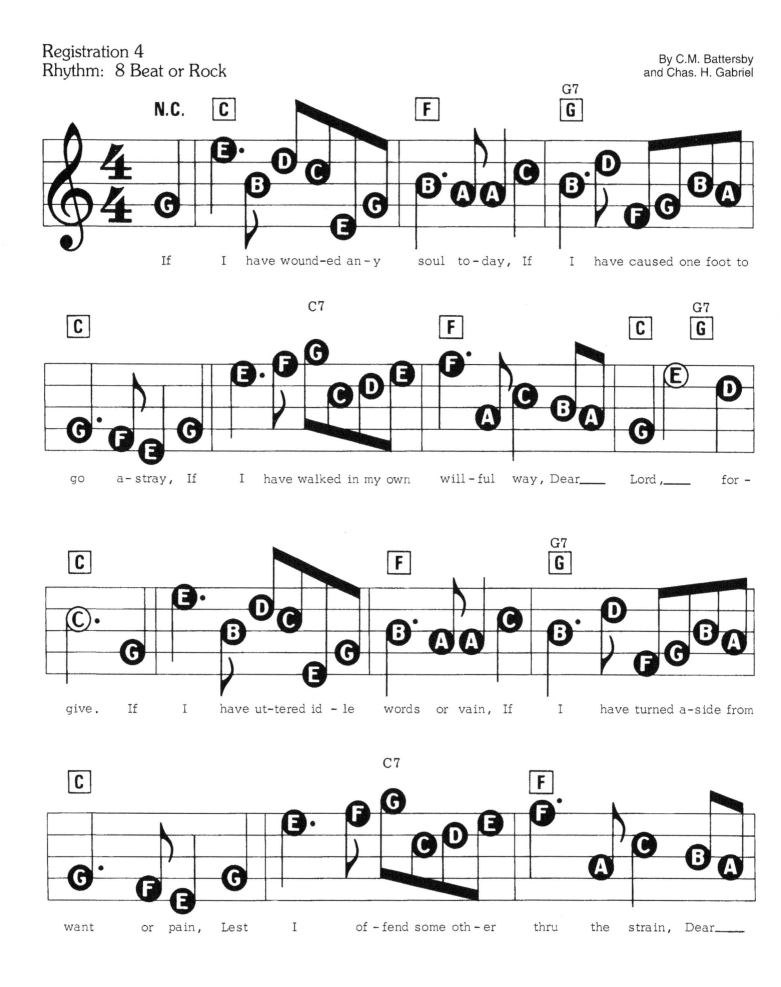

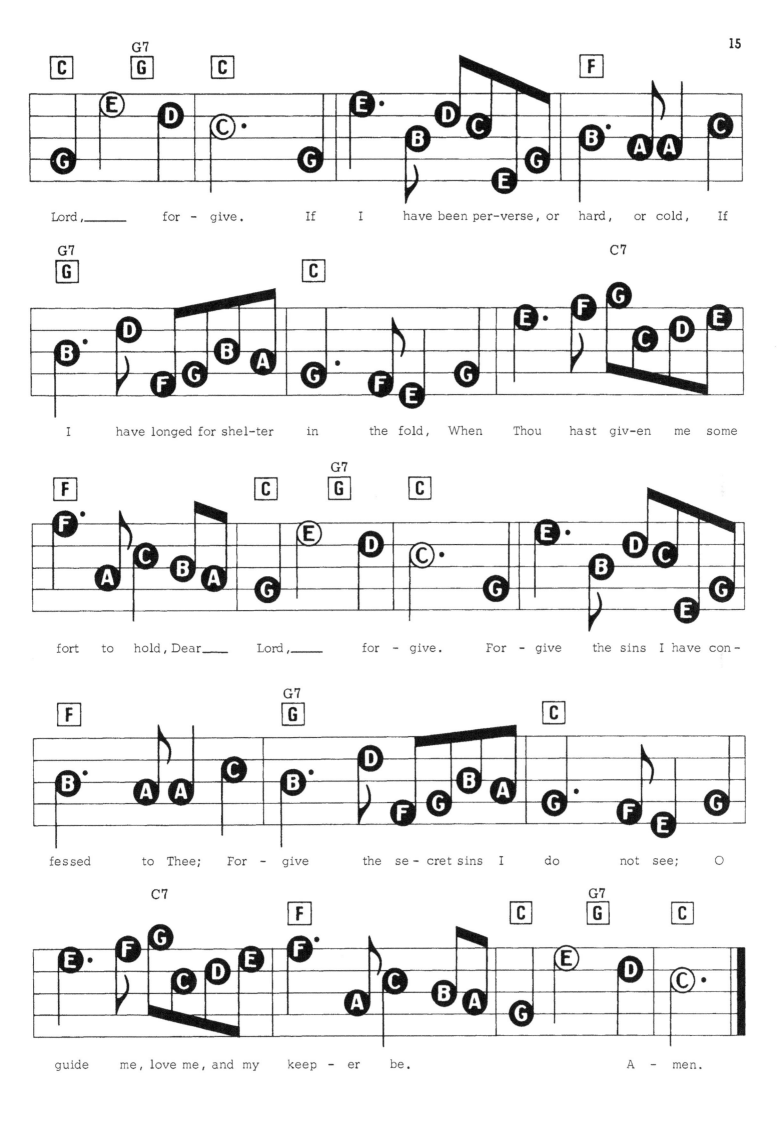

Farther Along

Registration 10
Rhythm: Waltz

Words and Music by J.R. Baxter, Jr.
and W.B. Stevens

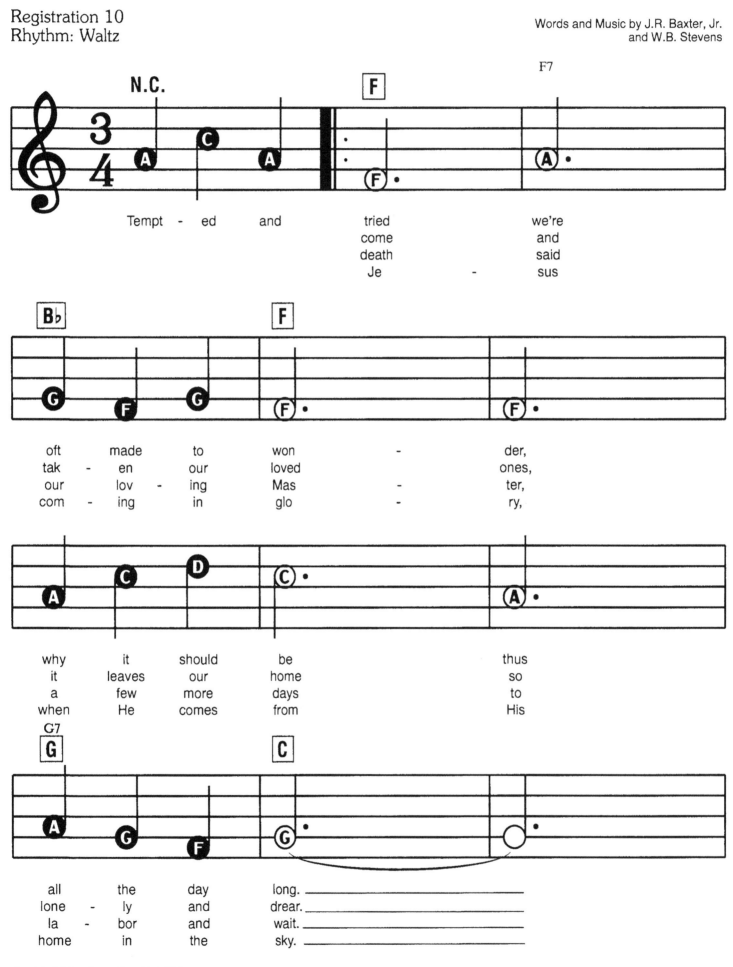

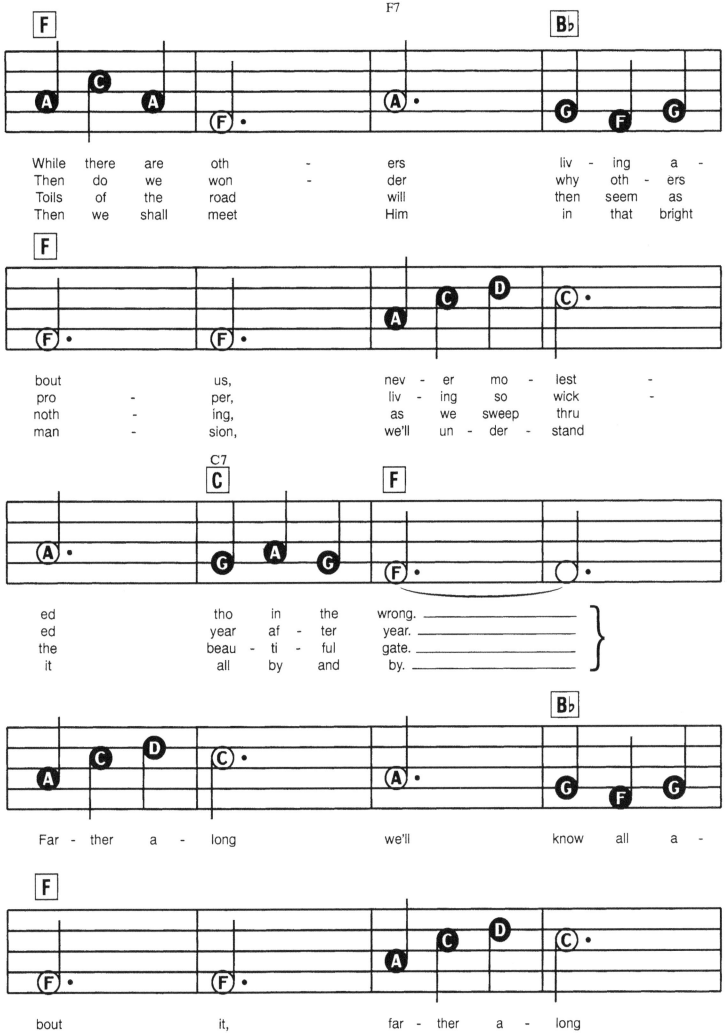

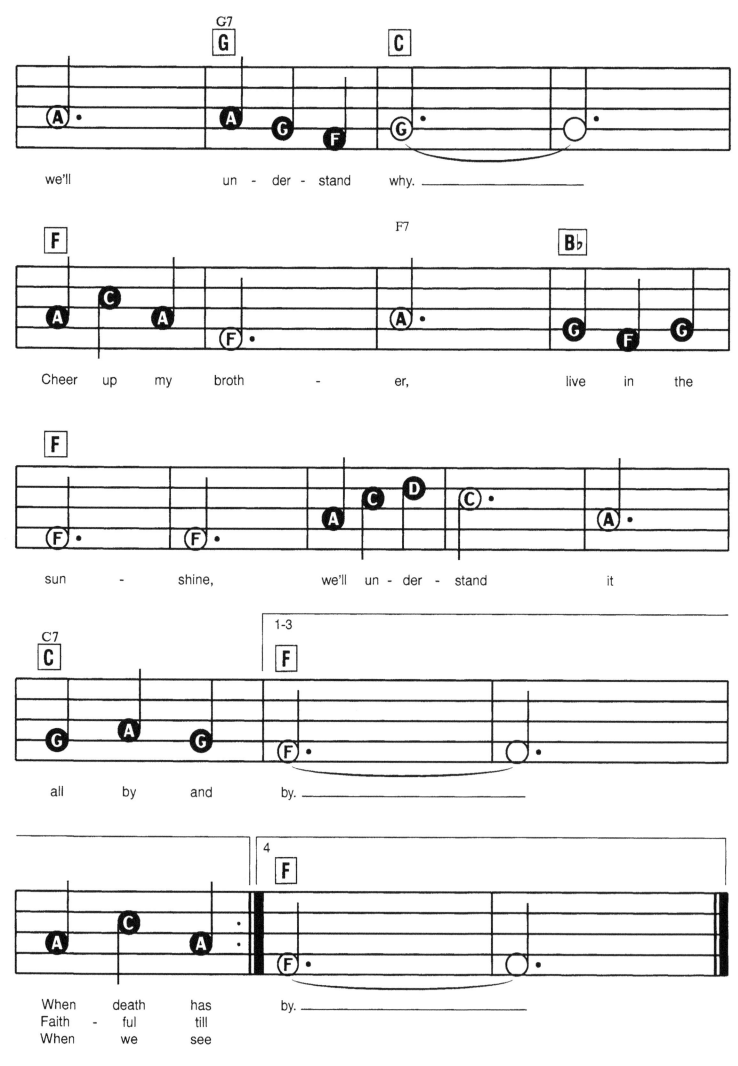

He Is My Everything

Registration 1
Rhythm: Waltz or Jazz Waltz

Words and Music by
Dallas Frazier

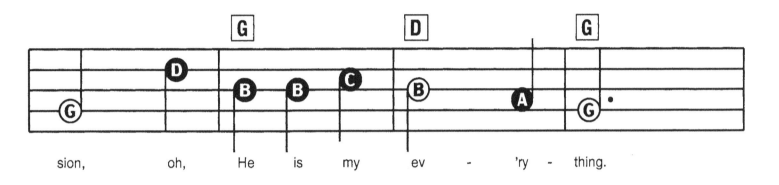

I long to be His pos - ses -

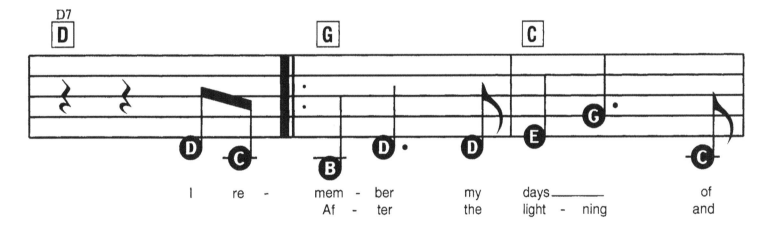

sion, oh, He is my ev - 'ry - thing.

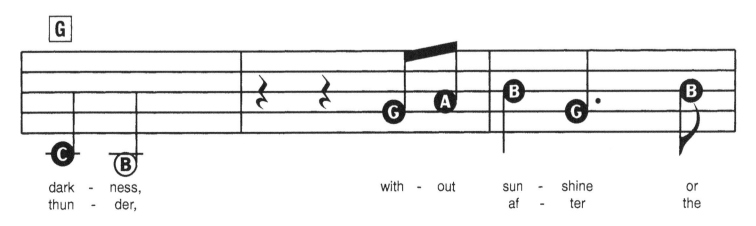

I re - mem - ber my days_____ of

Af - ter the light - ning and

dark - ness, with - out sun - shine or

thun - der, af - ter the

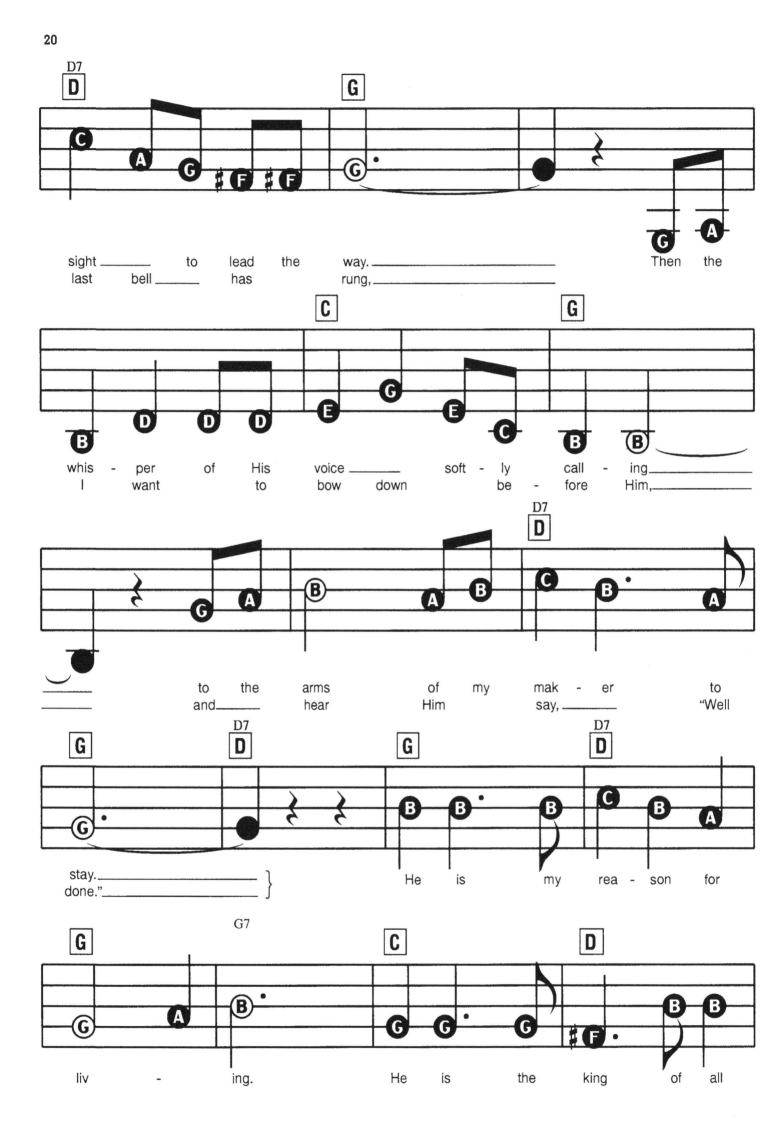

21

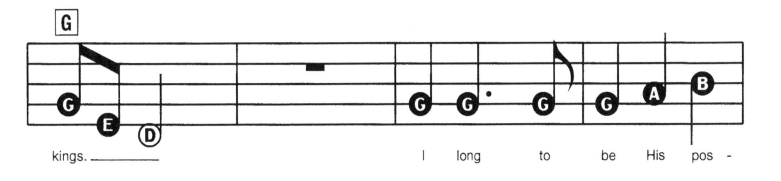

kings. _____ I long to be His pos -

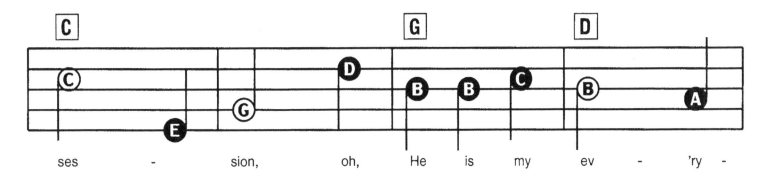

ses - sion, oh, He is my ev - 'ry -

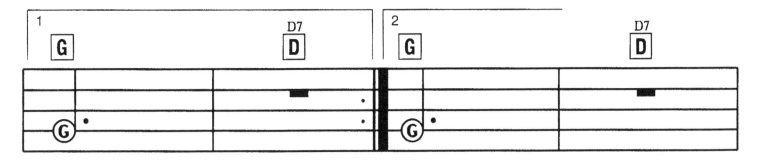

thing.   thing.

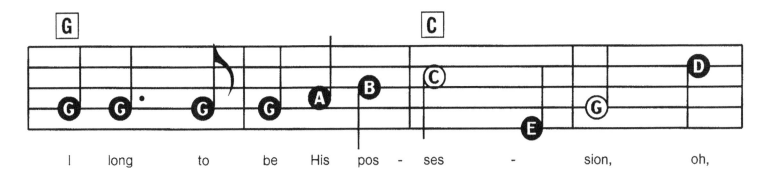

I long to be His pos - ses - sion, oh,

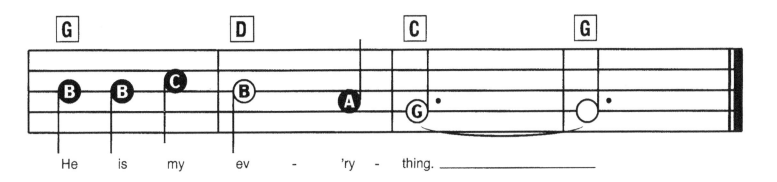

He is my ev - 'ry - thing. _____

He Touched Me

Registration 2
Rhythm: Waltz

Words and Music by
William J. Gaither

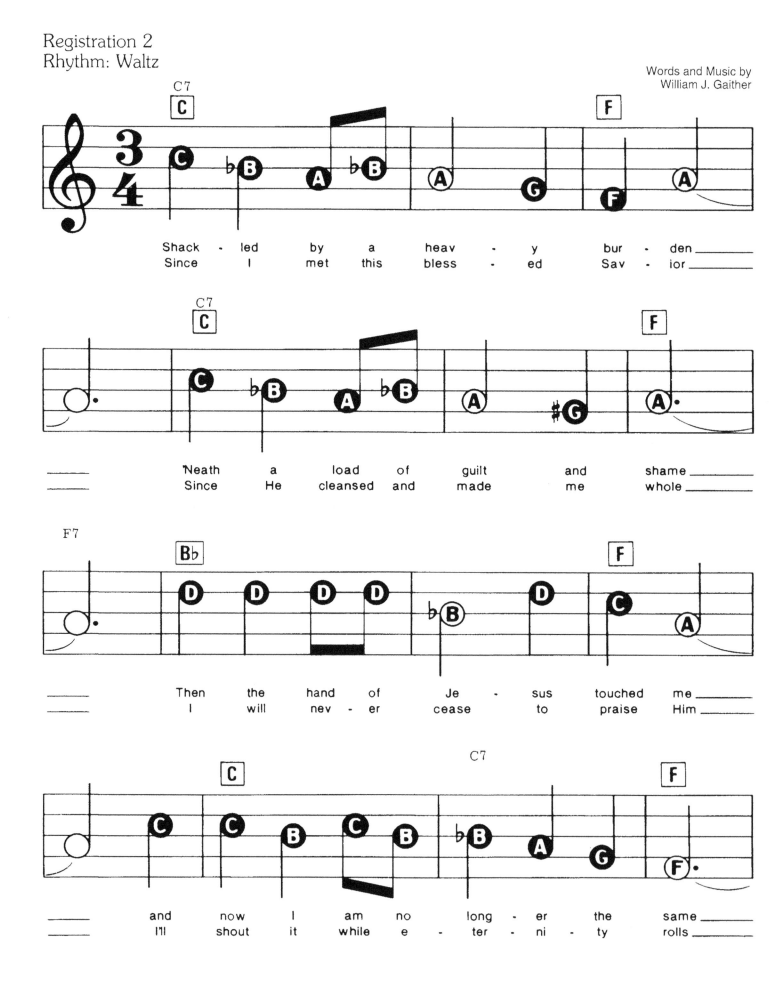

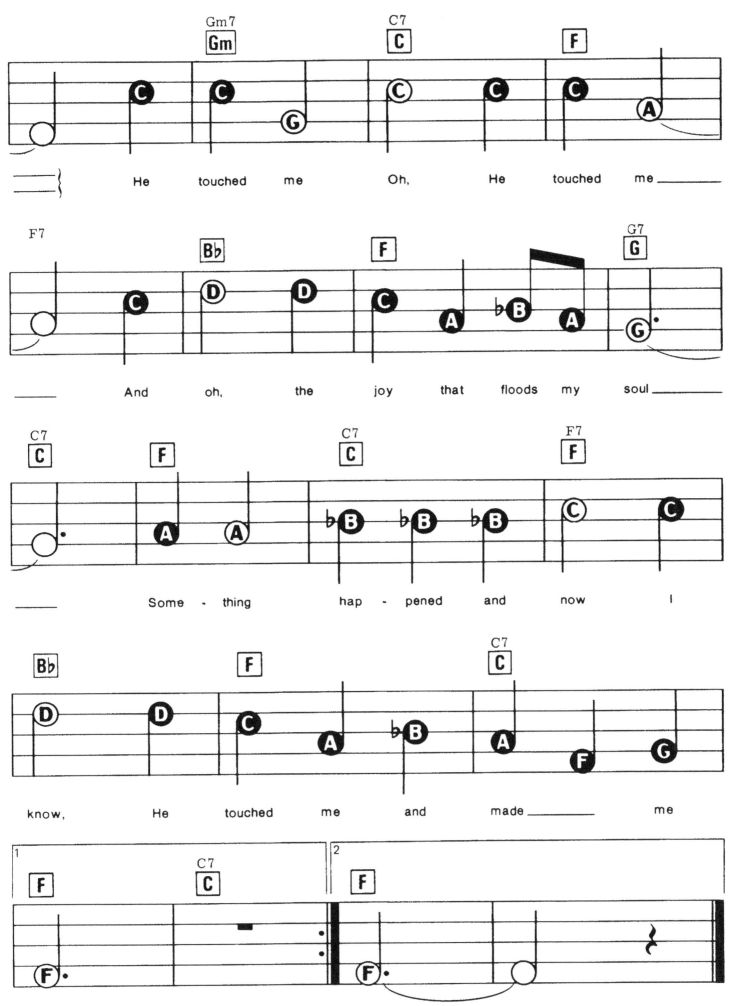

His Hand In Mine

Registration 8
Rhythm: Slow Rock or 6/8 March

Words and Music by
Mosie Lister

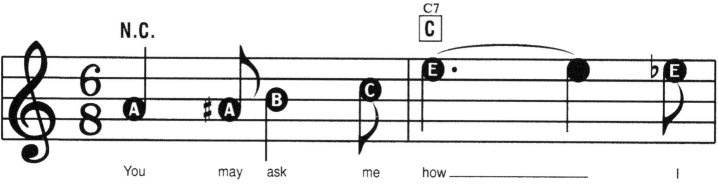

You   may ask   me   how _____   I

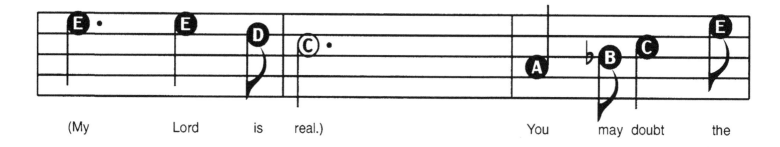

know   my   Lord   is   real.

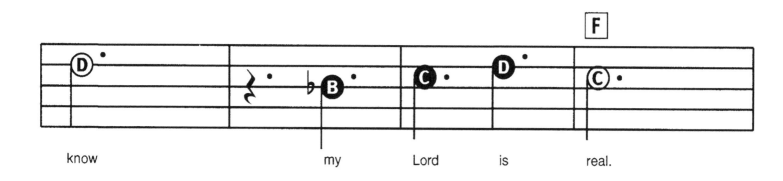

(My   Lord   is   real.)   You   may doubt   the

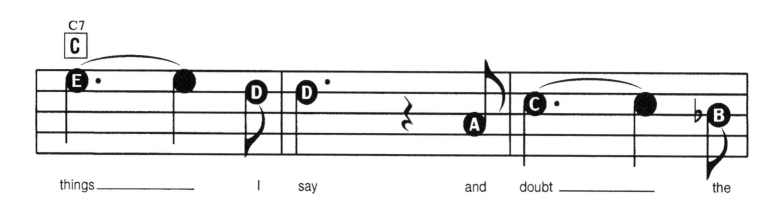

things _____   I   say   and   doubt _____   the

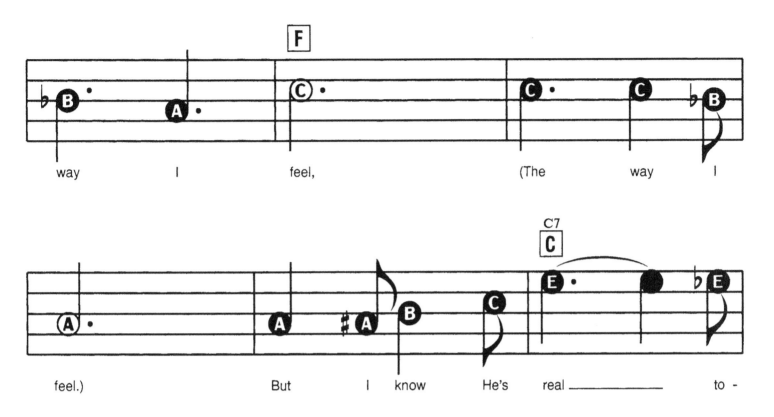

way   I   feel,   (The   way   I

feel.)   But   I   know   He's   real _____ to -

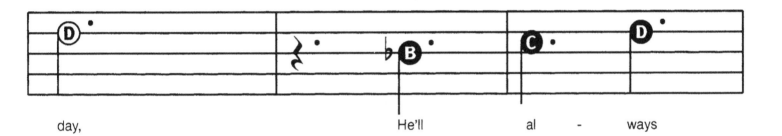

day,   He'll   al - ways

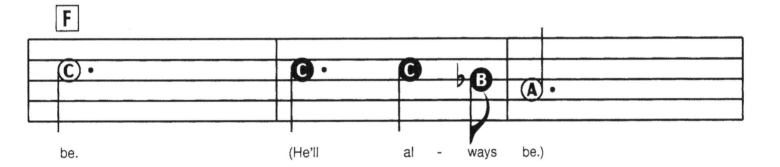

be.   (He'll   al - ways   be.)

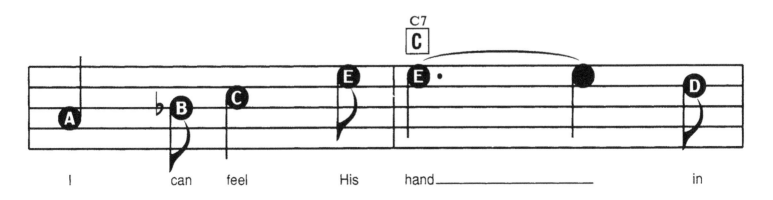

I   can   feel   His   hand _____ in

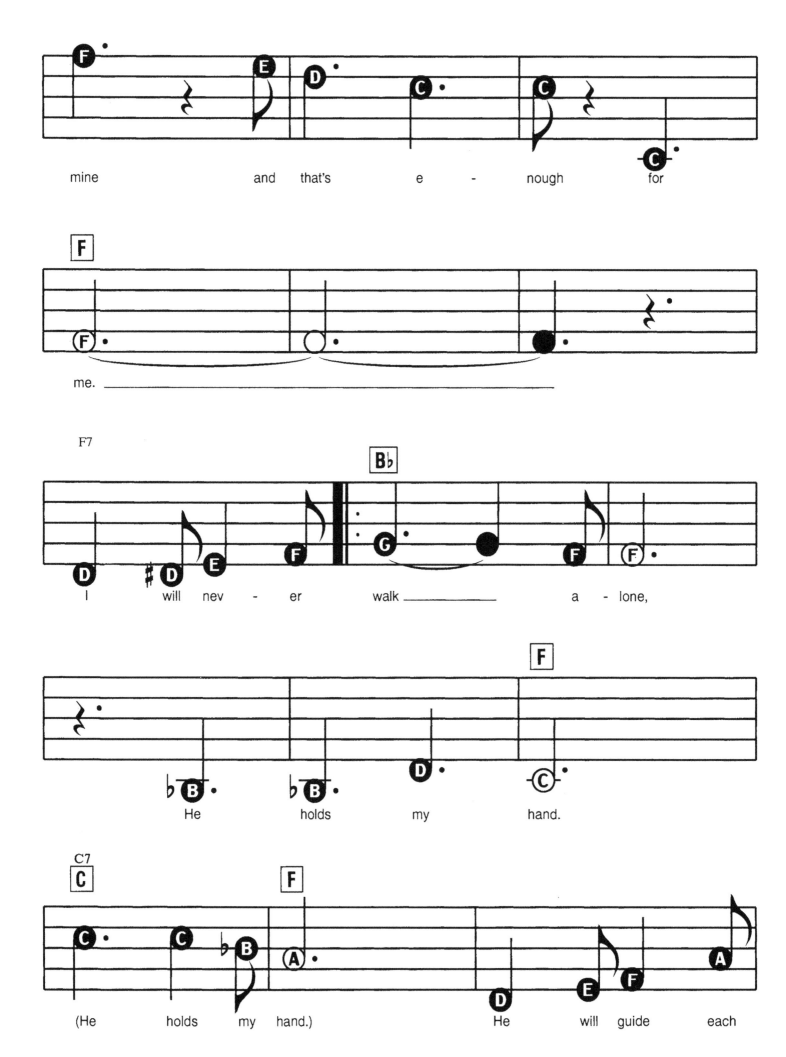

mine   and   that's   e - nough   for

me. _____

I   will nev - er   walk _____ a - lone,

He   holds   my   hand.

(He   holds   my   hand.)   He   will   guide   each

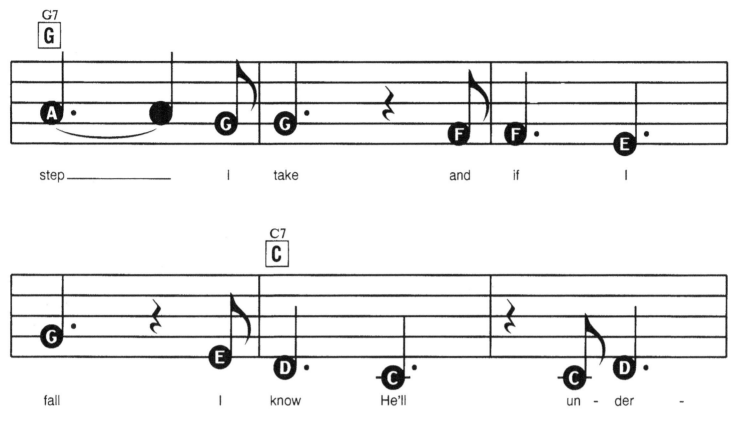

step _____ I take and if I

fall I know He'll un - der -

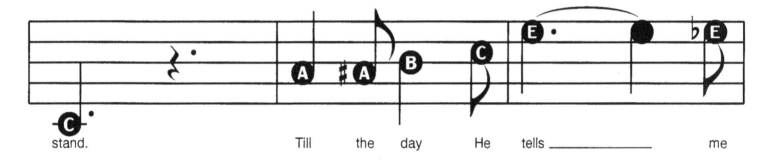

stand. Till the day He tells _____ me

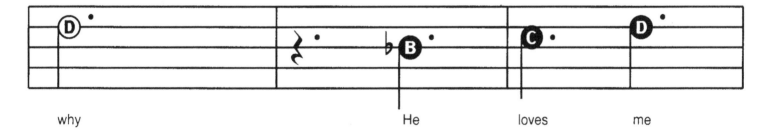

why He loves me

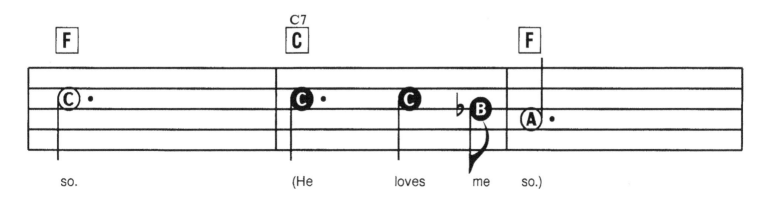

so. (He loves me so.)

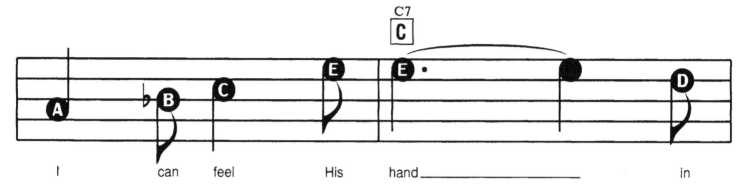

I can feel His hand _____ in

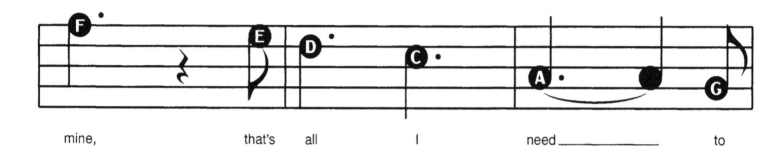

mine, that's all I need _____ to

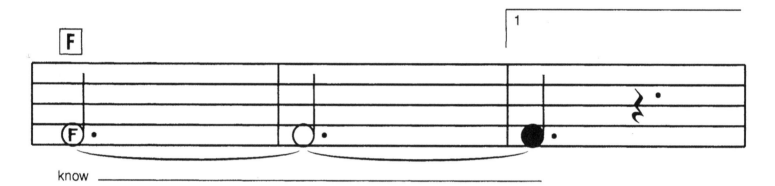

know _____

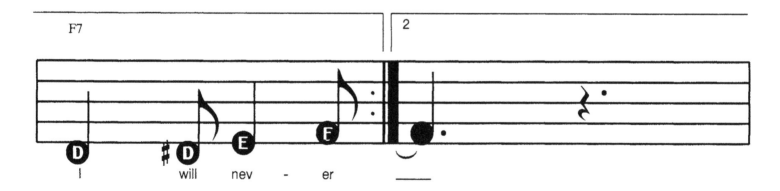

I will nev - er _____

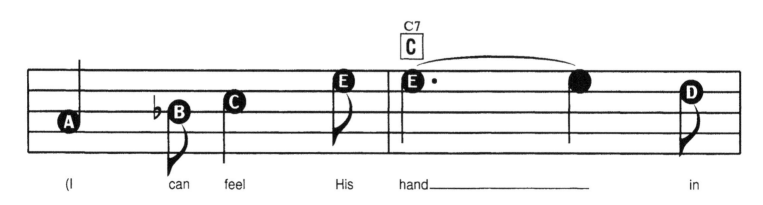

(I can feel His hand _____ in

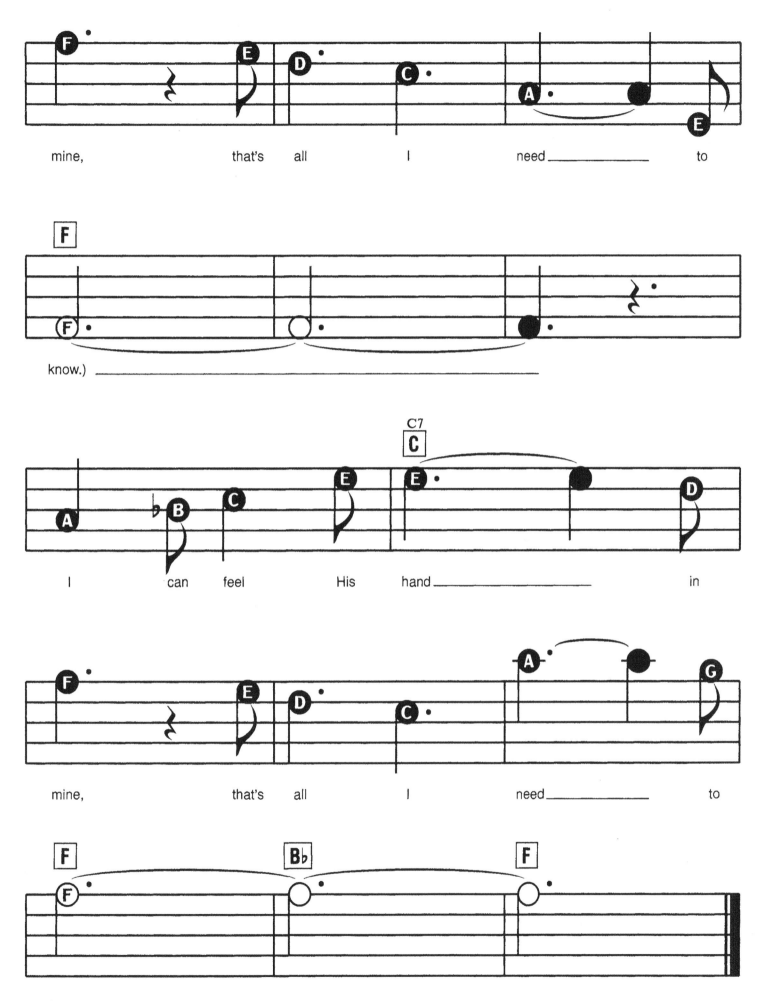

mine,   that's all   I   need _____ to

know.) _____

I   can feel   His   hand _____ in

mine,   that's all   I   need _____ to

know. _____

How Great Thou Art

Registration 2
Rhythm: 16 Beat or None

By Stuart K. Hine

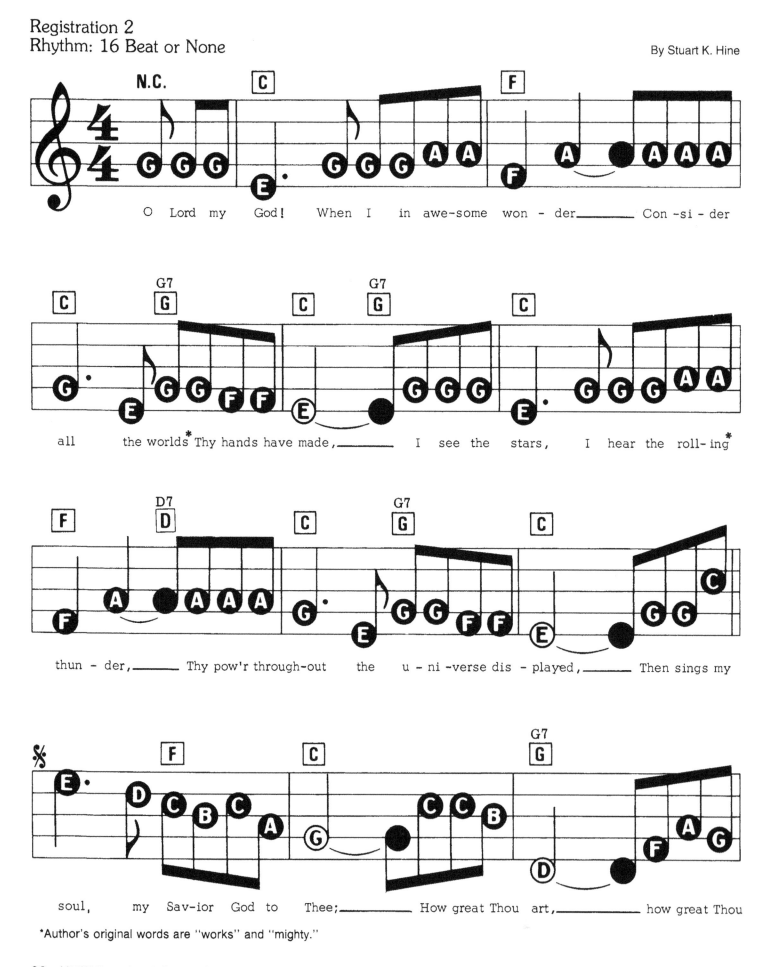

*Author's original words are "works" and "mighty."

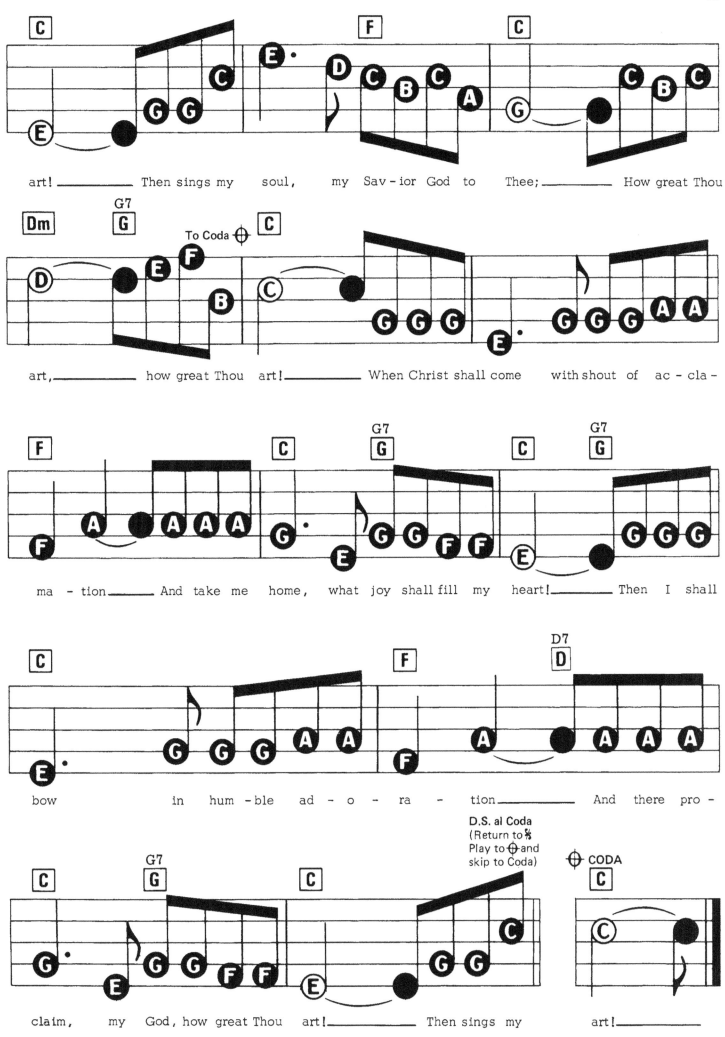

I Believe

Registration 2
Rhythm: Ballad or Slow Rock

Words and Music by Ervin Drake, Irvin Graham,
Jimmy Shirl and Al Stillman

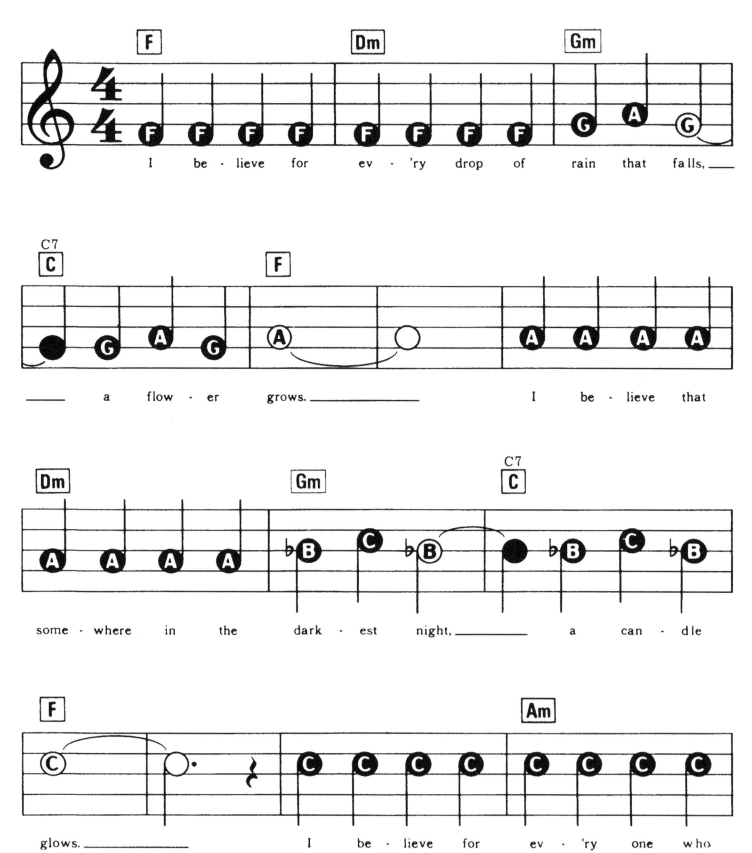

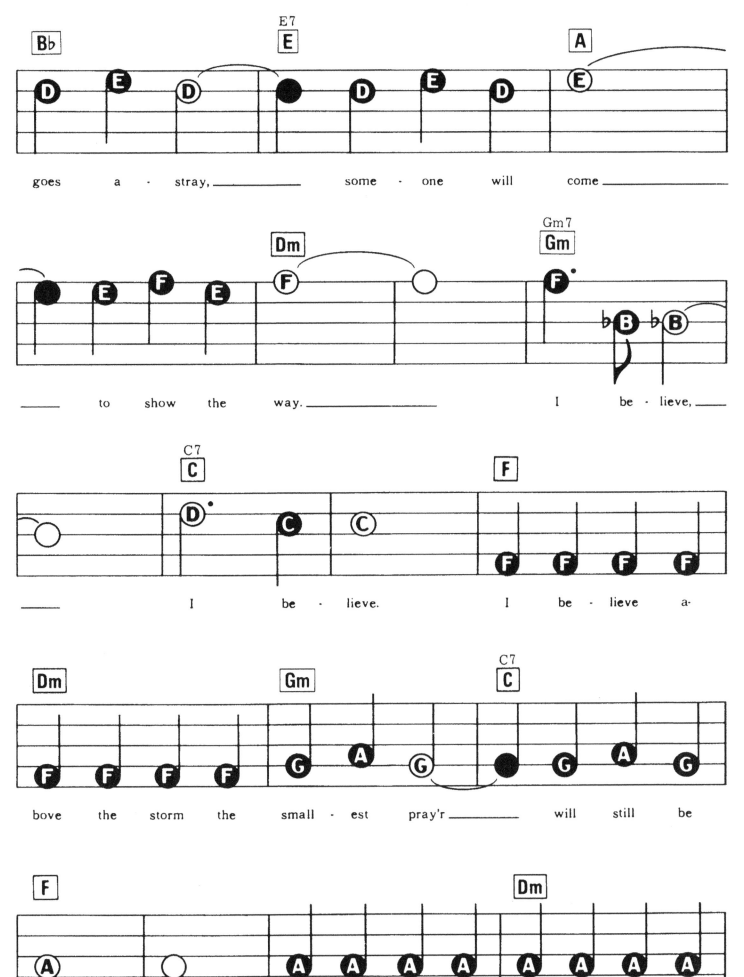

34

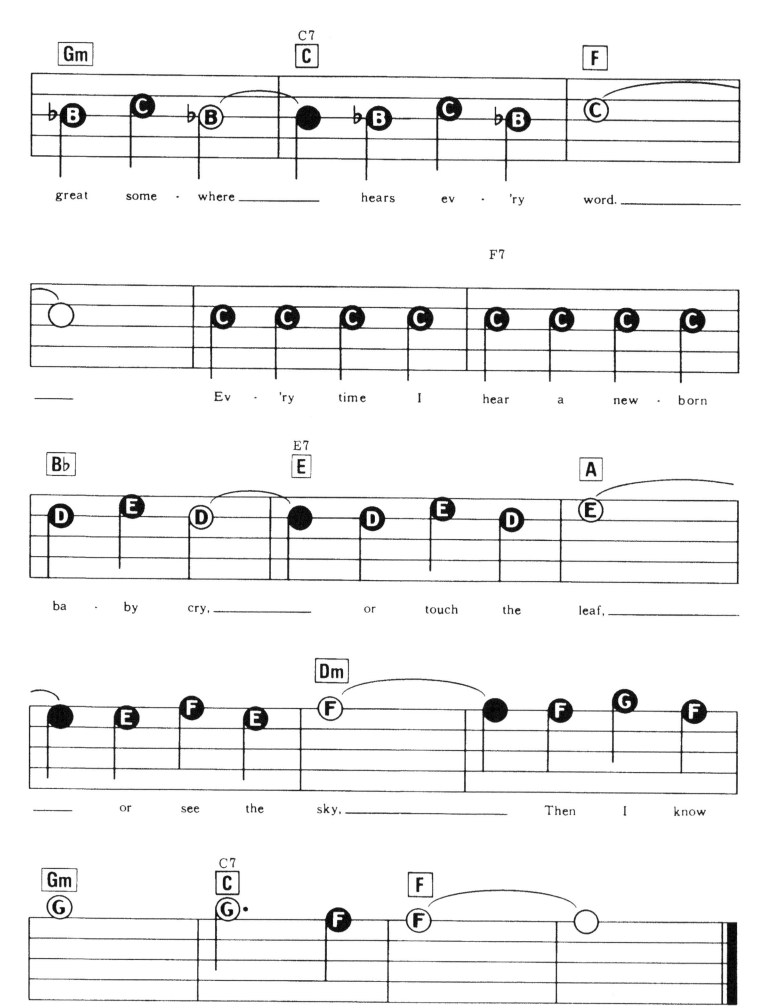

If That Isn't Love

Registration 10
Rhythm: Waltz

Words and Music by
Dottie Rambo

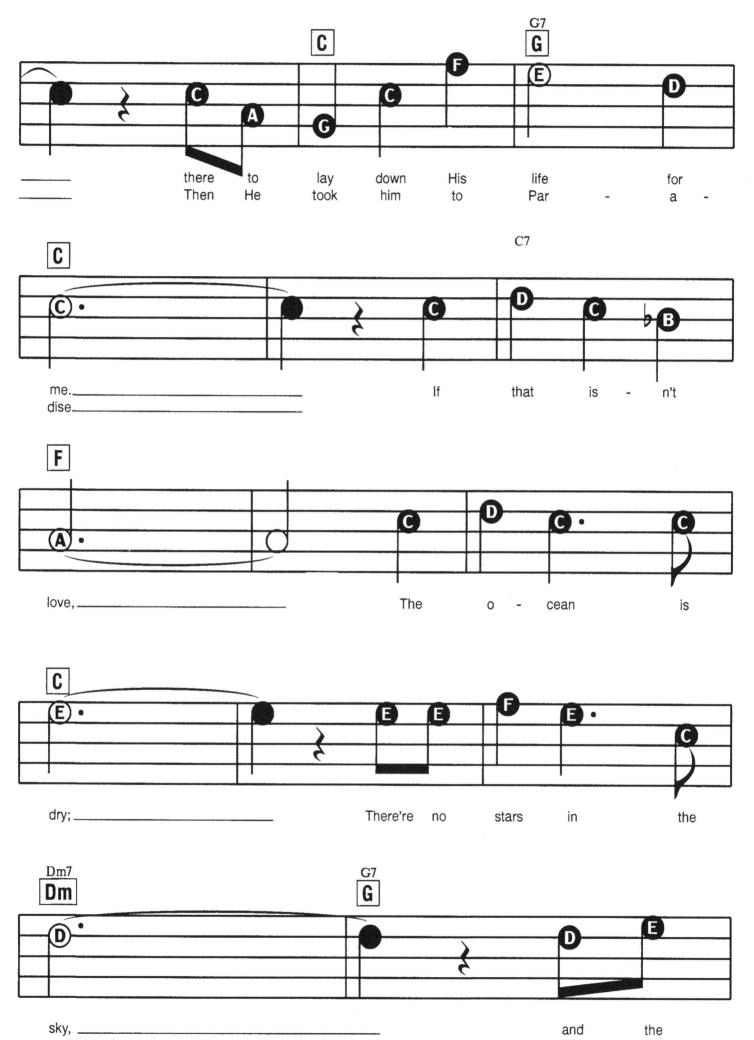

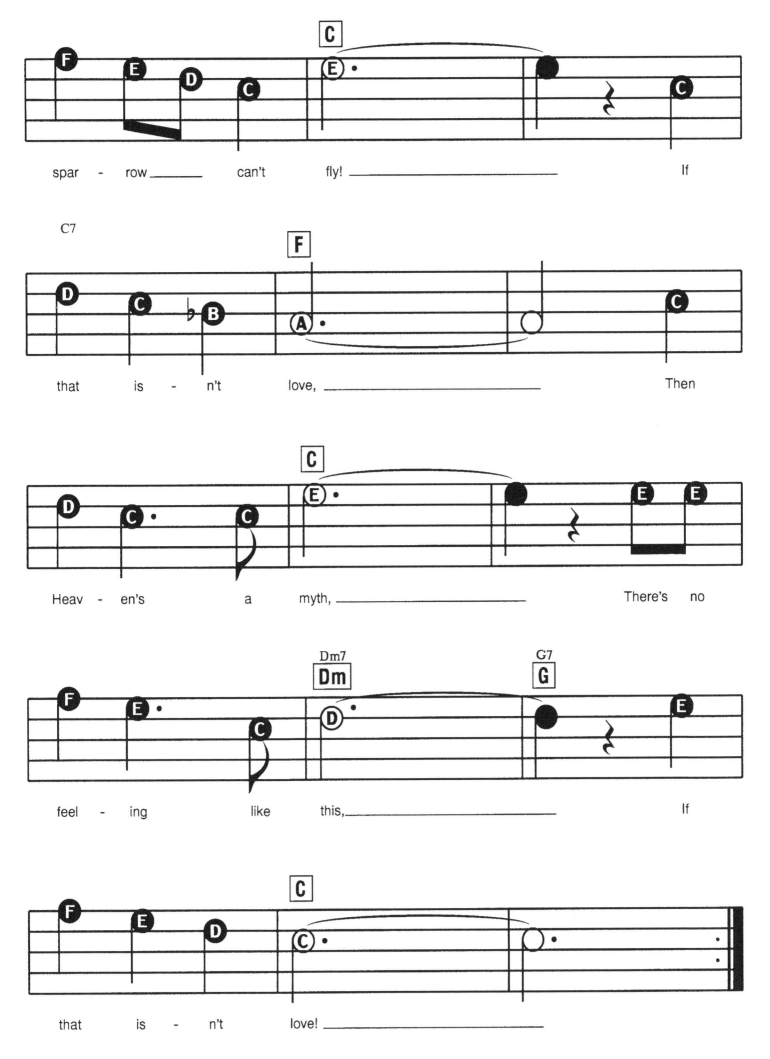

I Believe In The Man In The Sky

Registration 3
Rhythm: 8-Beat or Pops

Words and Music by
Richard Howard

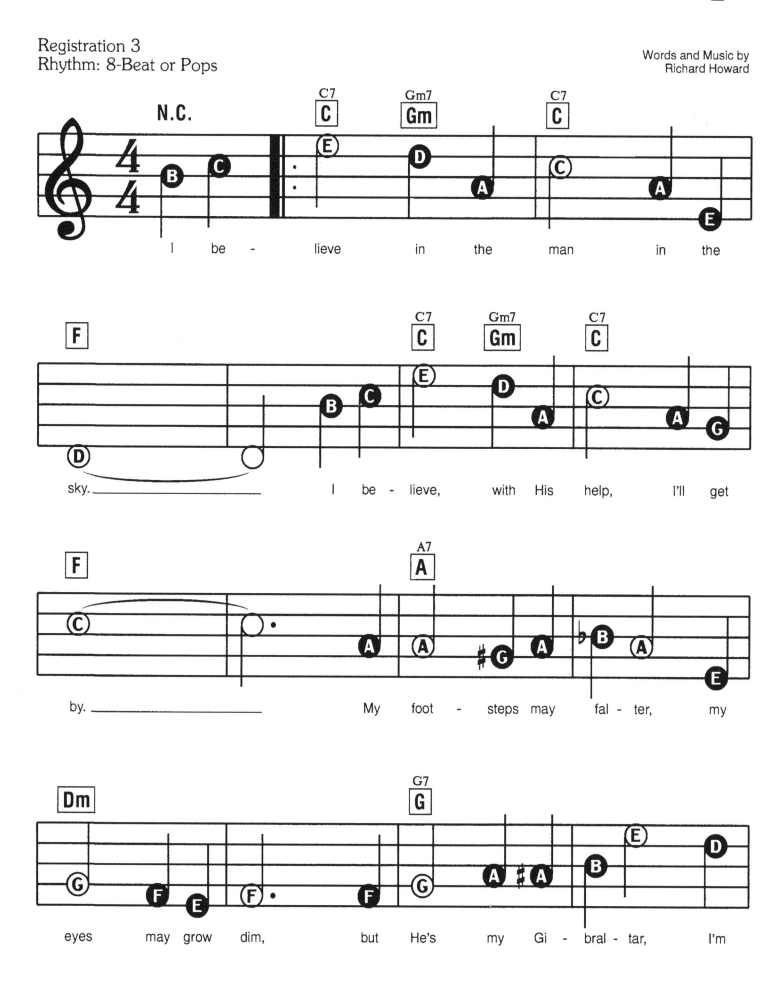

39

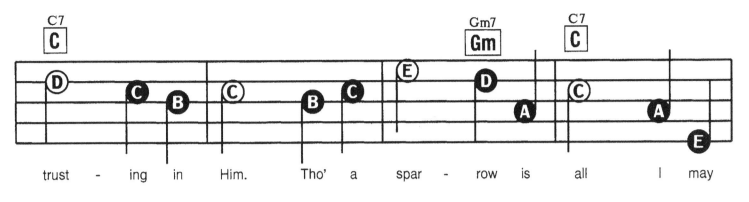

trust - ing in Him. Tho' a spar - row is all I may

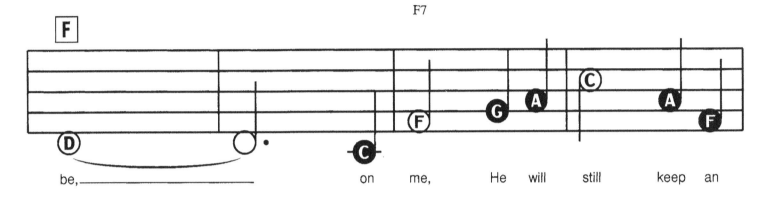

be, _____ on me, He will still keep an

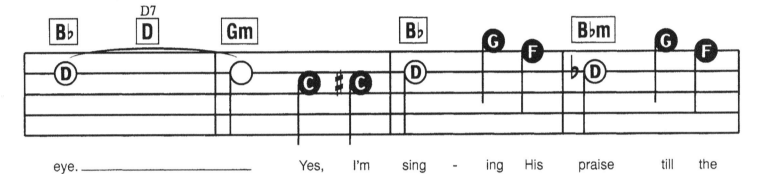

eye. _____ Yes, I'm sing - ing His praise till the

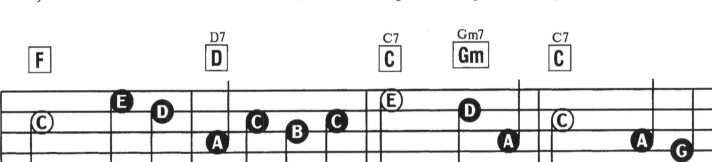

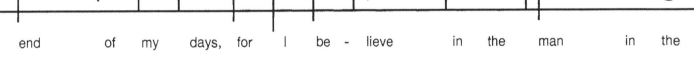

end of my days, for I be - lieve in the man in the

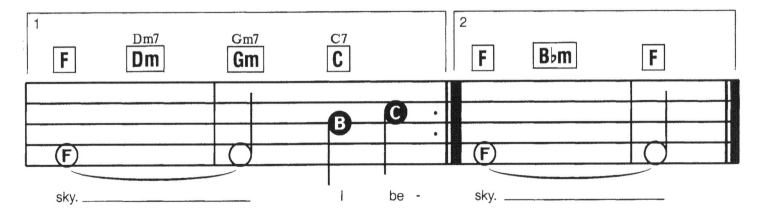

sky. _____ I be - sky. _____

I, John

Registration 4
Rhythm: March

Words and Music by William Johnson,
George McFadden and Ted Brooks

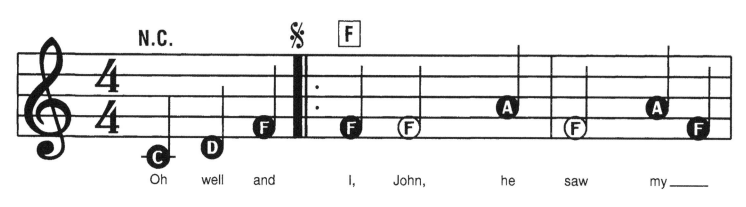

Oh well and I, John, he saw my _____

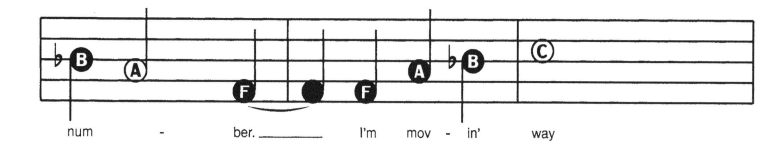

num - ber. _____ I'm mov - in' way

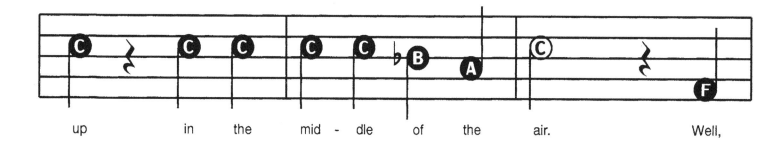

up in the mid - dle of the air. Well,

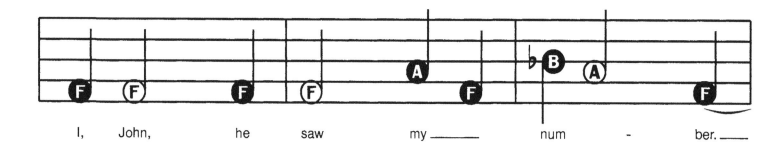

I, John, he saw my _____ num - ber. _____

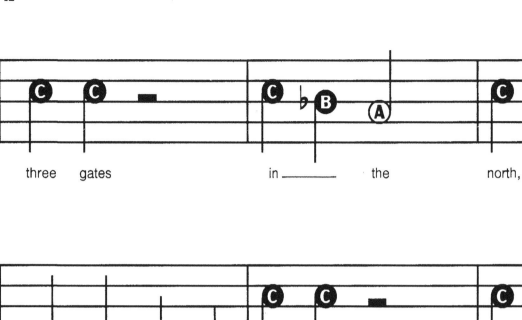

three gates   in _____ the   north, ha - le -

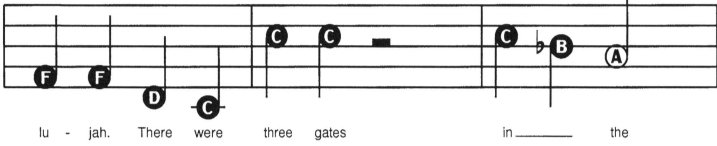

lu - jah. There were   three gates   in _____ the

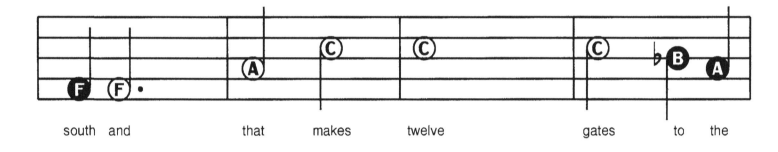

south and   that makes twelve   gates   to   the

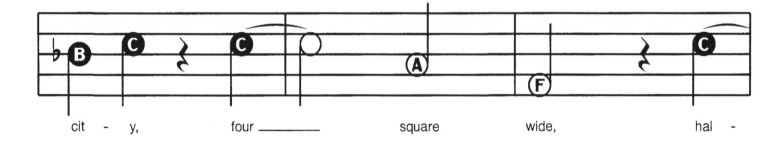

cit - y,   four _____ square   wide,   hal -

D.S. al Coda
(Return to %
Play to ⊕ and
Skip to Coda)

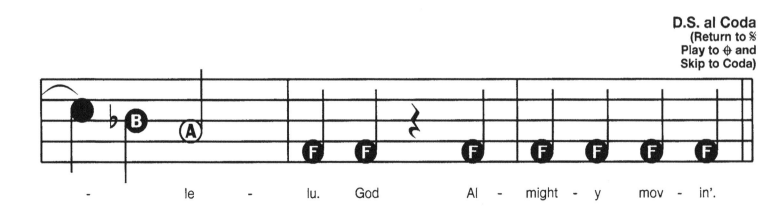

- le - lu. God   Al - might - y mov - in'.

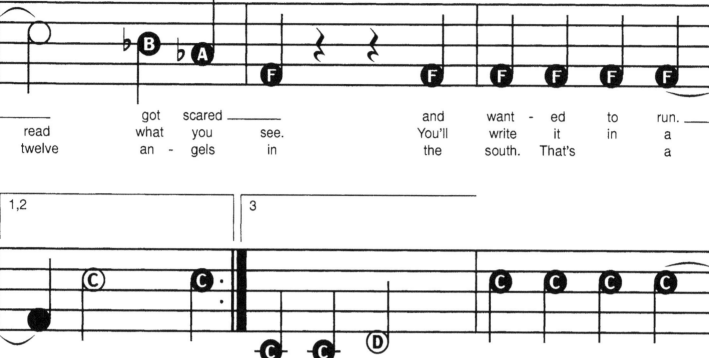

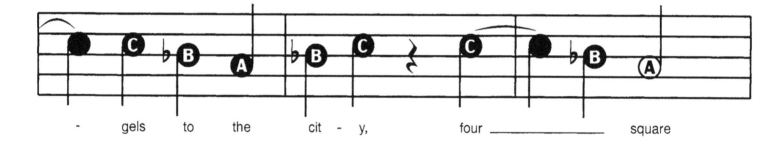

got scared _____ and want - ed to run. ___
read what you see. You'll write it in a
twelve an - gels in the south. That's a

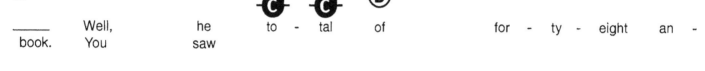

1,2 | 3

_____ Well, he to - tal of for - ty - eight an -
book. You saw

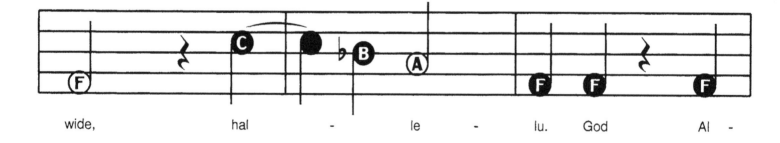

- gels to the cit - y, four _____ square

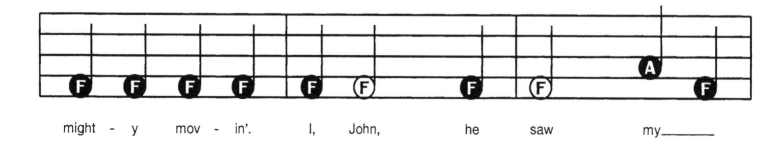

wide, hal - le - lu. God Al -

might - y mov - in'. I, John, he saw my_____

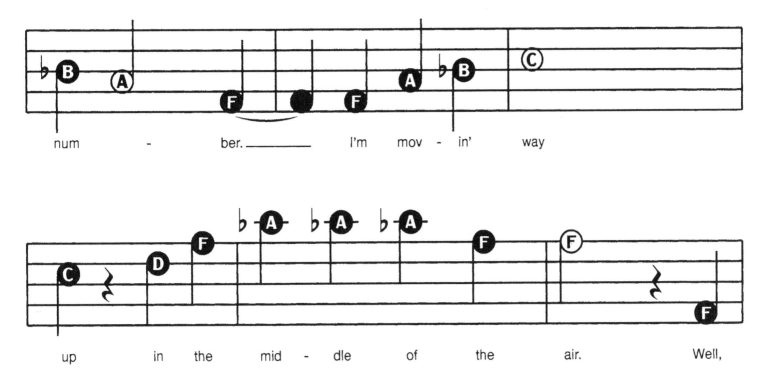

num - ber._____ I'm mov - in' way

up in the mid - dle of the air. Well,

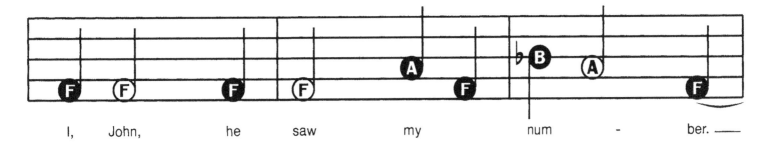

I, John, he saw my num - ber.___

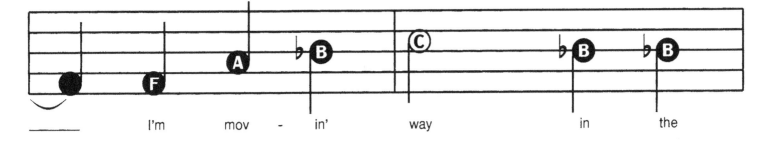

___ I'm mov - in' way in the

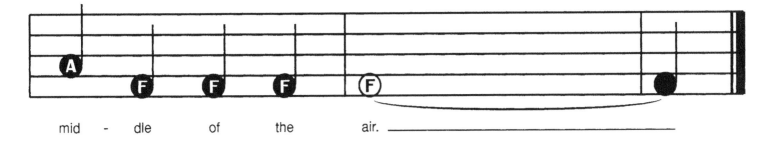

mid - dle of the air. _____

If I Can Dream

Registration 9
Rhythm: Slow Rock

Words and Music by
W. Earl Brown

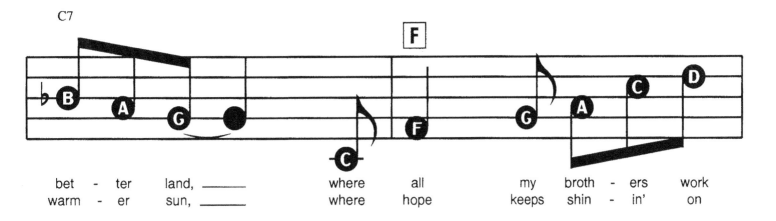

bet - ter land, _____ where all my broth - ers work
warm - er sun, _____ where hope keeps shin - in' on

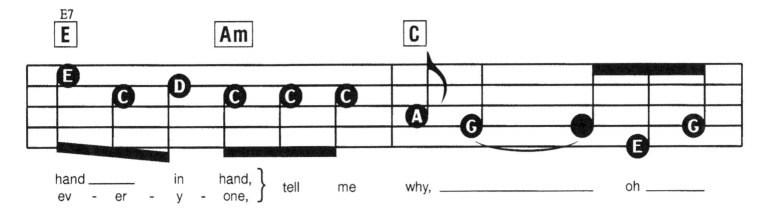

hand _____ in hand, } tell me why, _____ oh _____
ev - er - y - one,

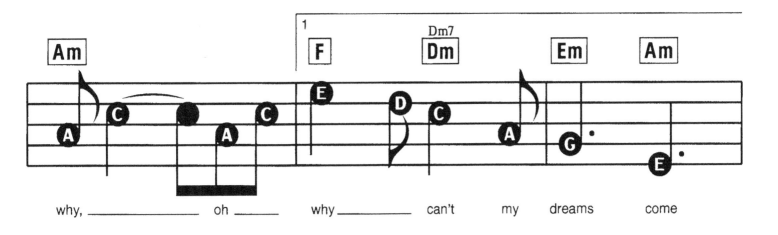

why, _____ oh _____ why _____ can't my dreams come

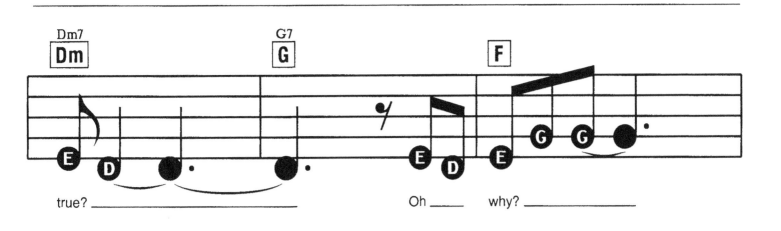

true? _____ Oh _____ why? _____

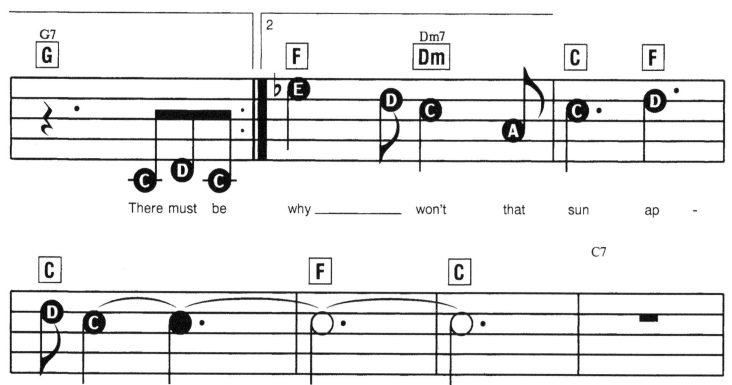

There must be   why _____ won't   that sun ap -

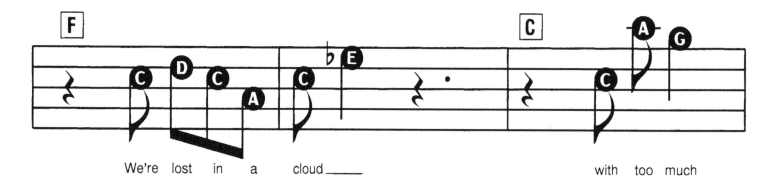

pear? _____

We're lost in a   cloud____   with too much

rain, _____   we're trapped in a   world ____

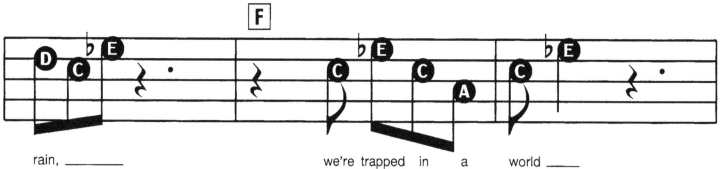

that's trou - bled with   pain, _____

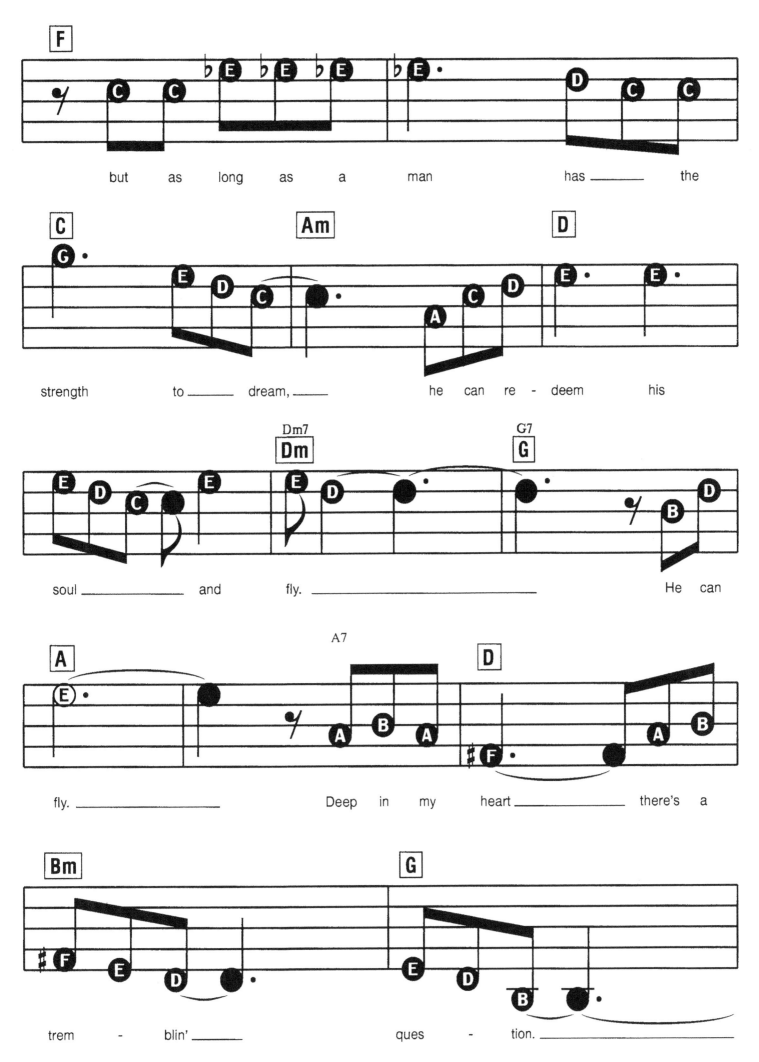

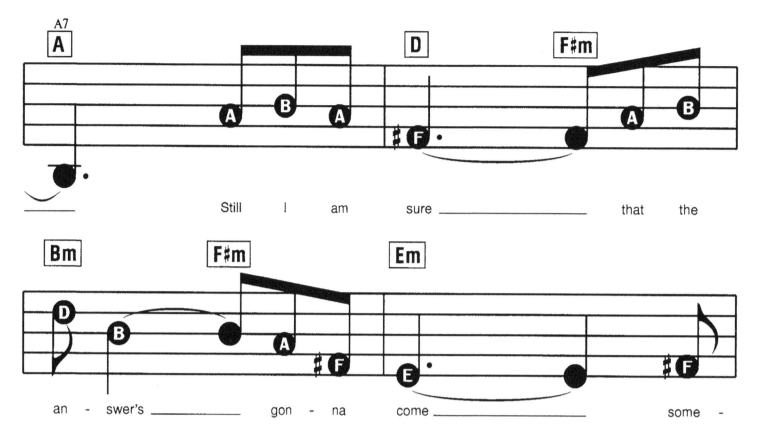

Still I am sure _____ that the

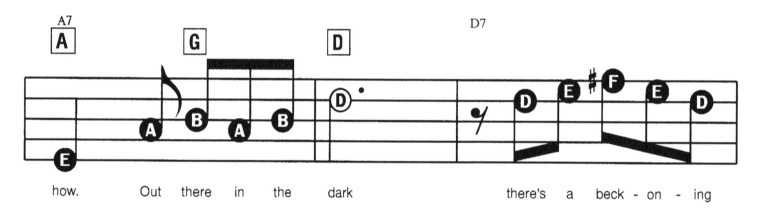

an - swer's _____ gon - na come _____ some -

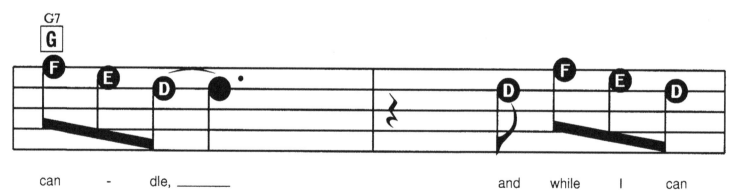

how. Out there in the dark there's a beck - on - ing

can - dle, _____ and while I can

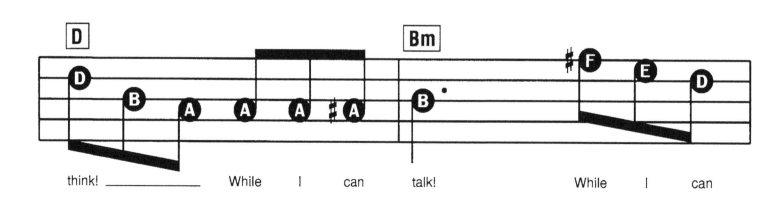

think! _____ While I can talk! While I can

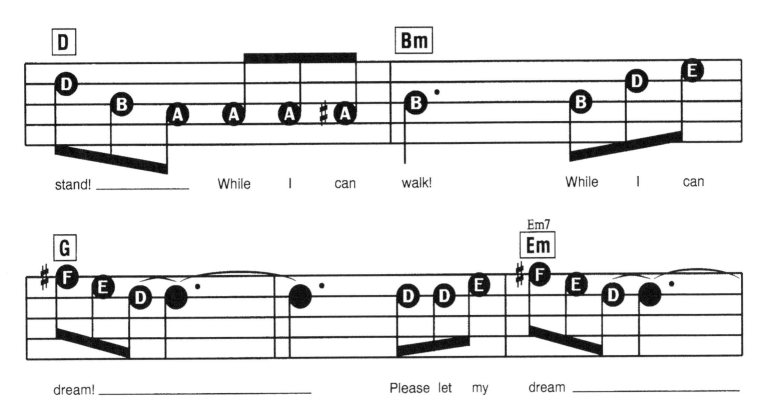

stand! _____ While I can walk! While I can

dream! _____ Please let my dream _____

____ come true _____

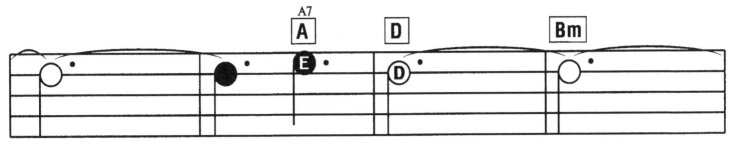

_____ right now! _____

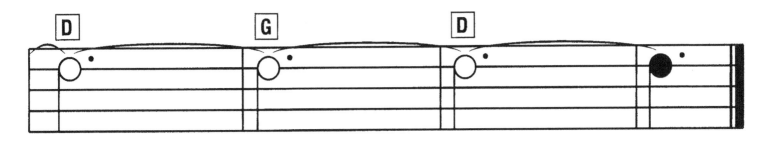

If The Lord Wasn't Walking By My Side

Registration 9
Rhythm: Swing or Shuffle

Words and Music by
Henry Slaughter

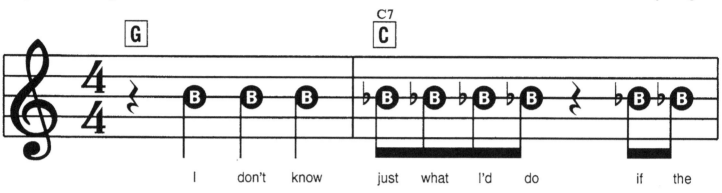

I don't know just what I'd do if the

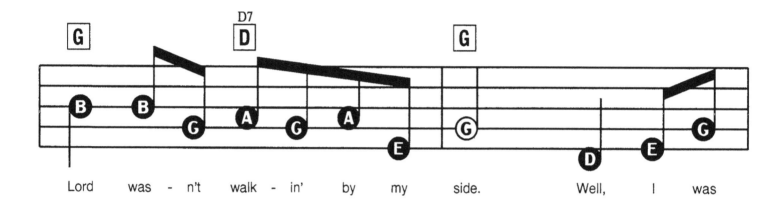

Lord was - n't walk - in' by my side. Well, I was

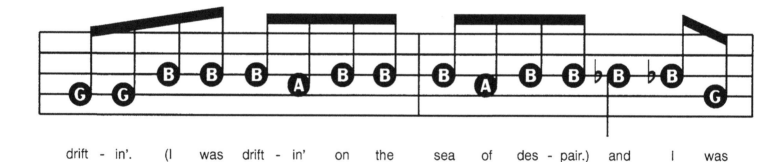

drift - in'. (I was drift - in' on the sea of des - pair.) and I was

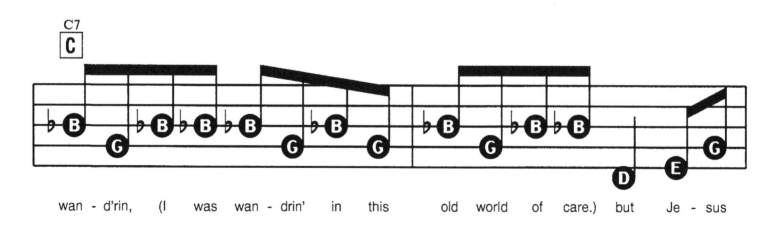

wan - d'rin, (I was wan - drin' in this old world of care.) but Je - sus

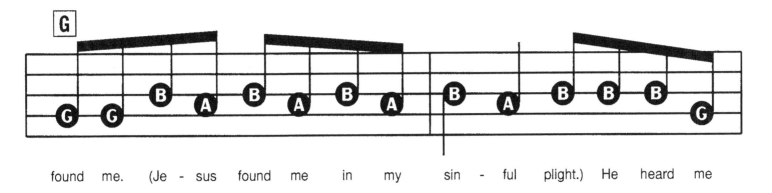

found me. (Je - sus found me in my sin - ful plight.) He heard me

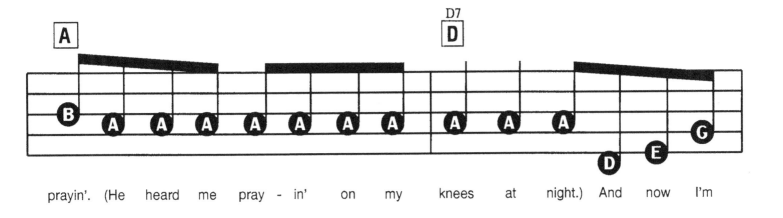

prayin'. (He heard me pray - in' on my knees at night.) And now I'm

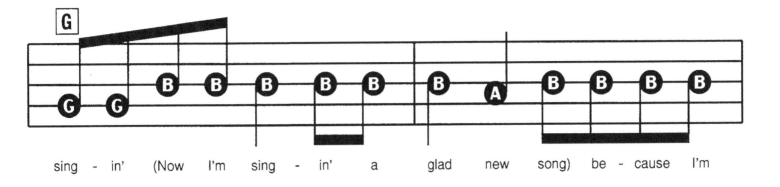

sing - in' (Now I'm sing - in' a glad new song) be - cause I'm

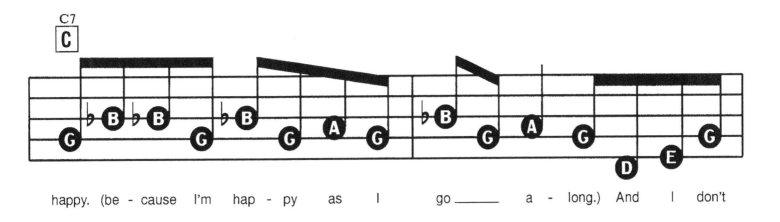

happy. (be - cause I'm hap - py as I go _____ a - long.) And I don't

54

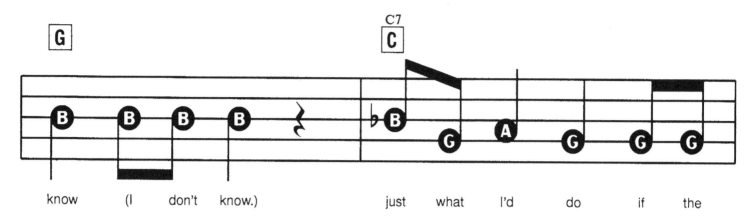

know (I don't know.) just what I'd do if the

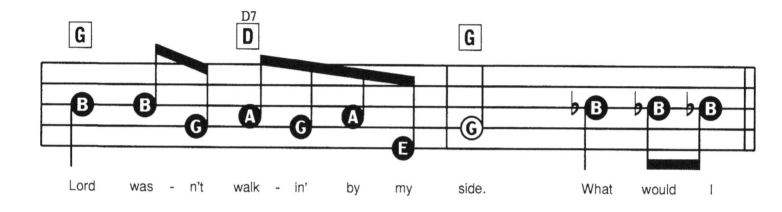

Lord was - n't walk - in' by my side. What would I

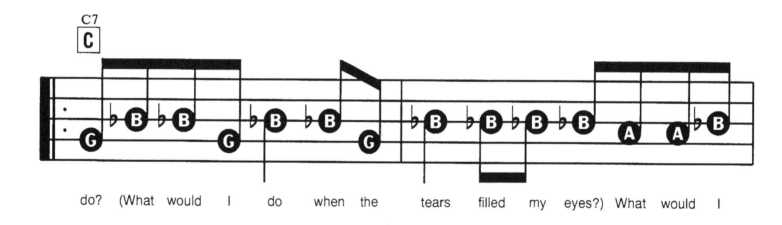

do? (What would I do when the tears filled my eyes?) What would I

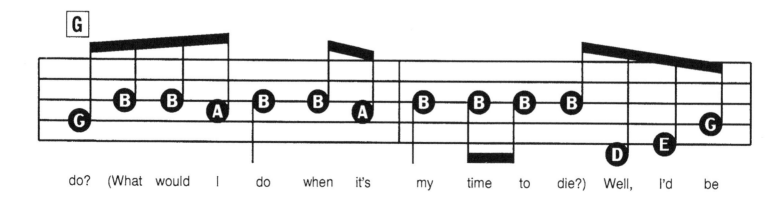

do? (What would I do when it's my time to die?) Well, I'd be

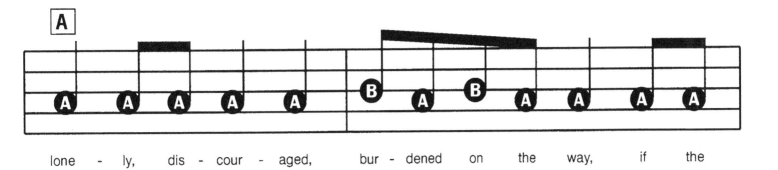

lone - ly, dis - cour - aged, bur - dened on the way, if the

D7

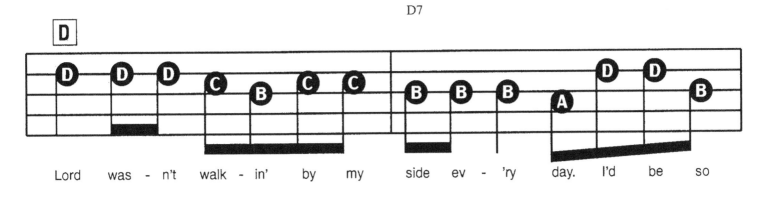

Lord was - n't walk - in' by my side ev - 'ry day. I'd be so

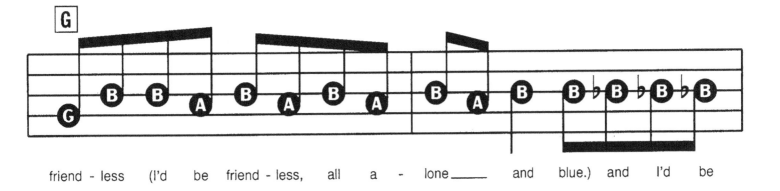

friend - less (I'd be friend - less, all a - lone___ and blue.) and I'd be

C7

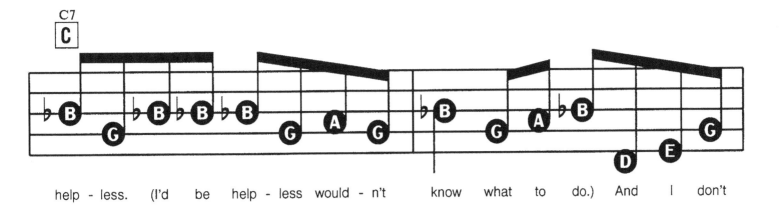

help - less. (I'd be help - less would - n't know what to do.) And I don't

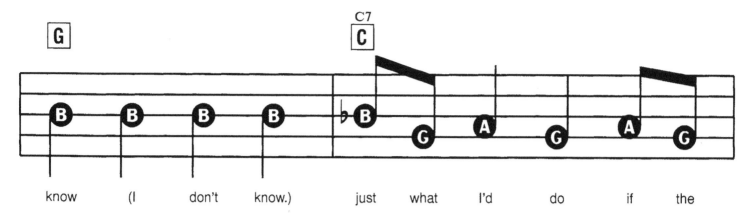

know (I don't know.) just what I'd do if the

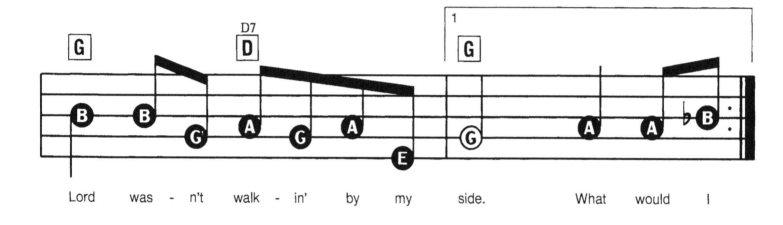

Lord was - n't walk - in' by my side. What would I

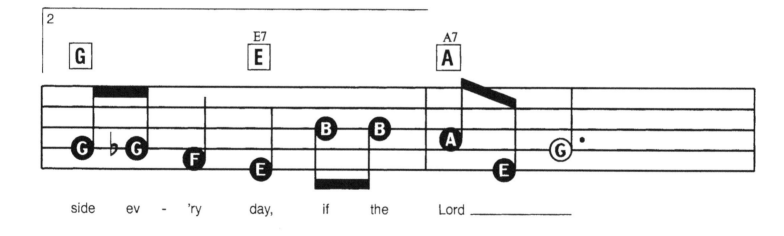

side ev - 'ry day, if the Lord _____

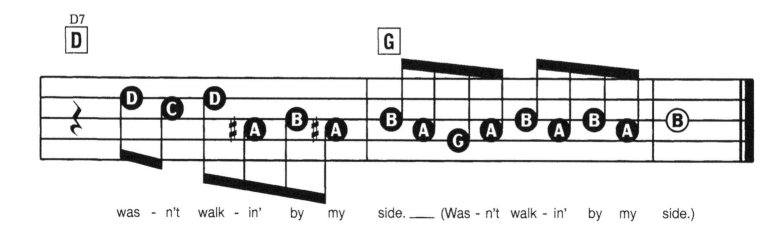

was - n't walk - in' by my side. ___ (Was - n't walk - in' by my side.)

Let Us Pray

Registration 4
Rhythm: Rock or Pops

Words by Buddy Kaye
Music by Ben Weisman

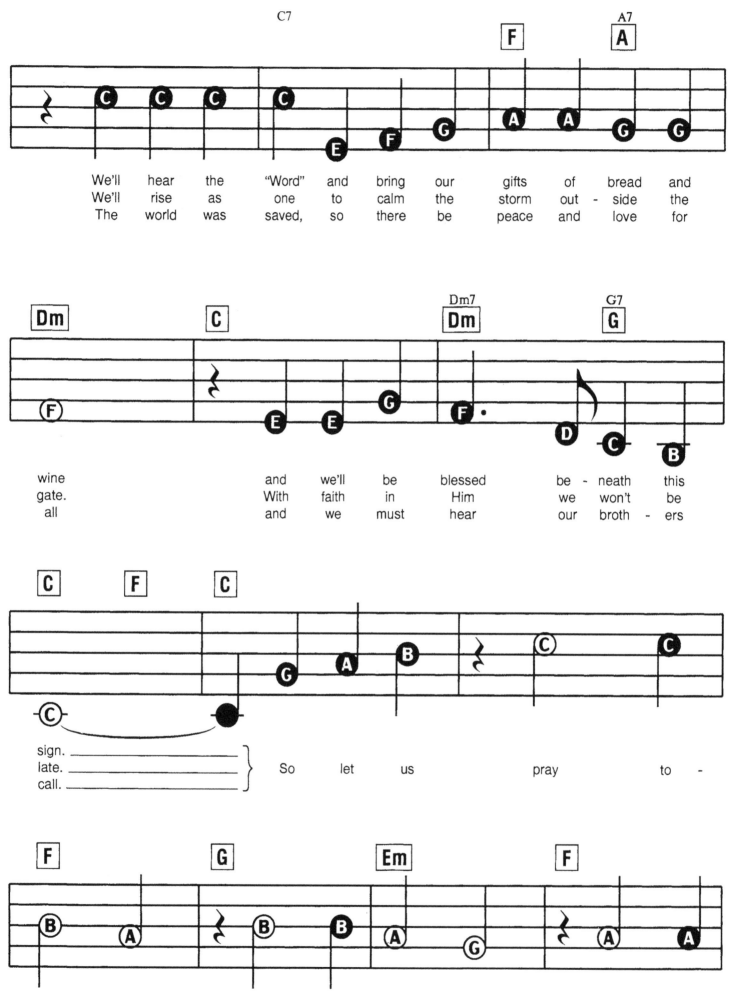

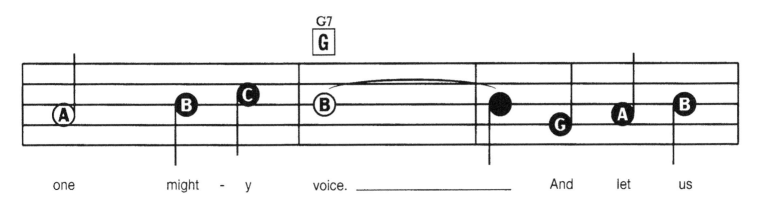

one might - y voice. _____ And let us

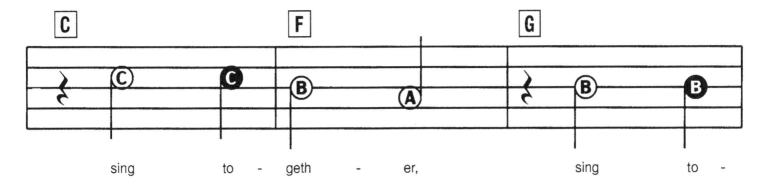

sing to - geth - er, sing to -

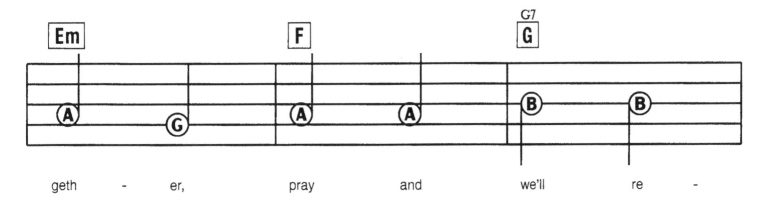

geth - er, pray and we'll re -

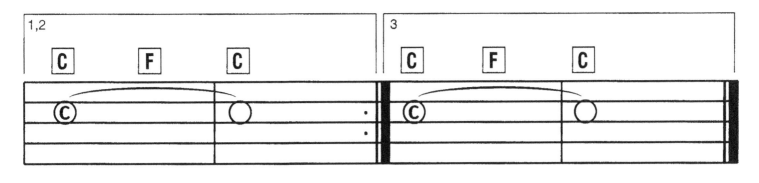

joice. _____ joice. _____

Joshua Fit The Battle

Registration 6
Rhythm: Swing or Shuffle

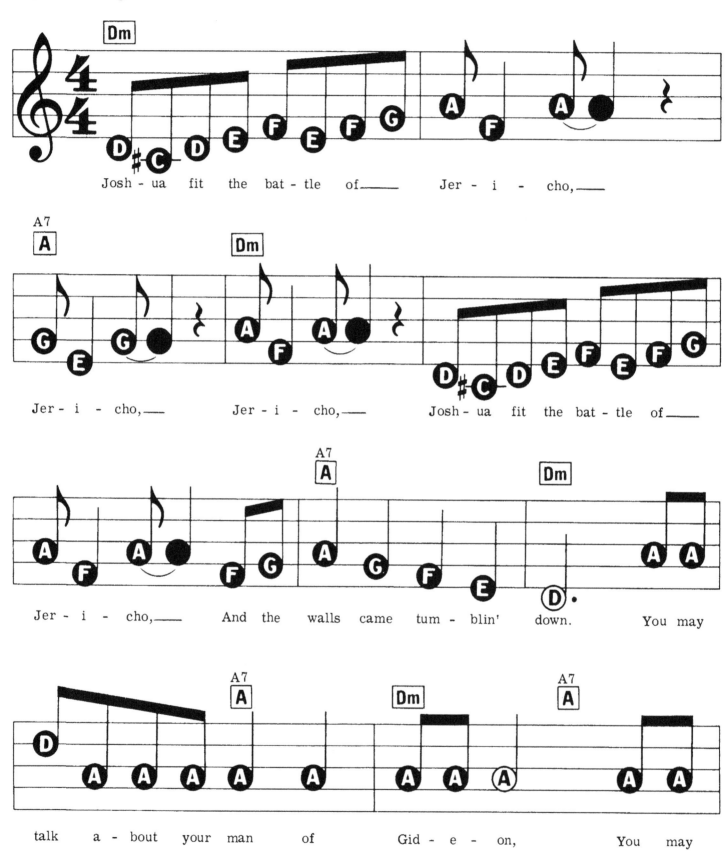

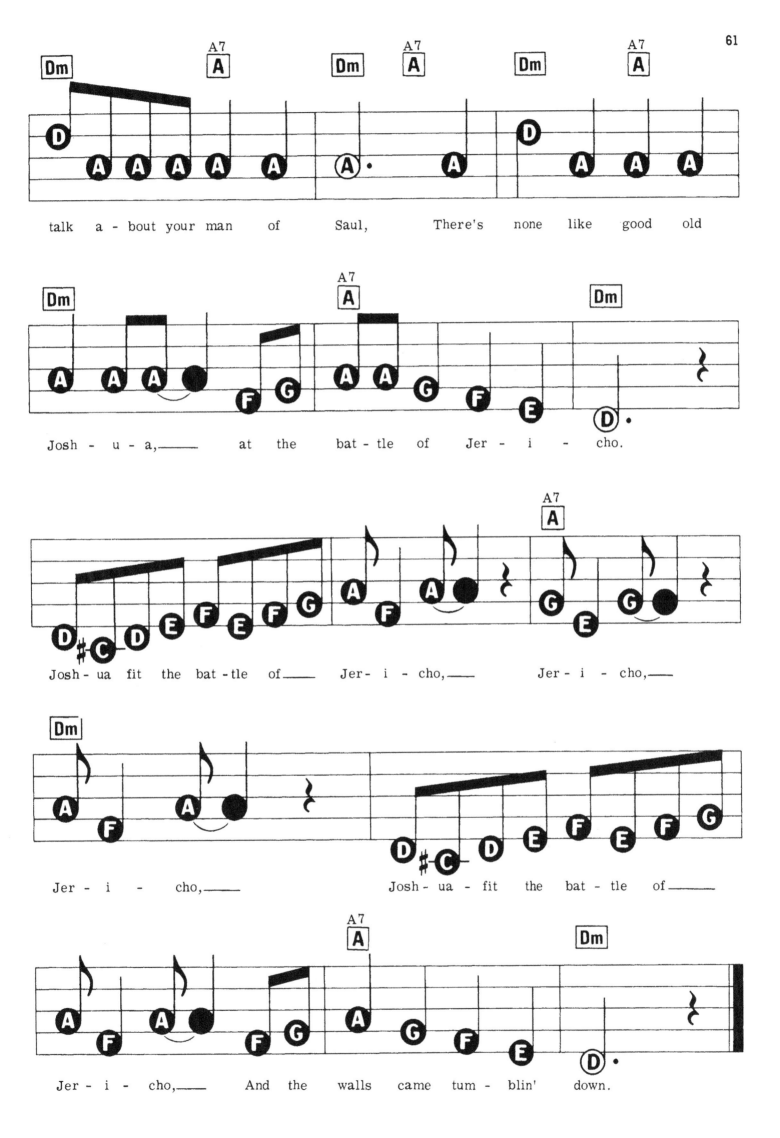

Lead Me, Guide Me

Registration 2
Rhythm: Waltz

Words and Music by
Doris Akers

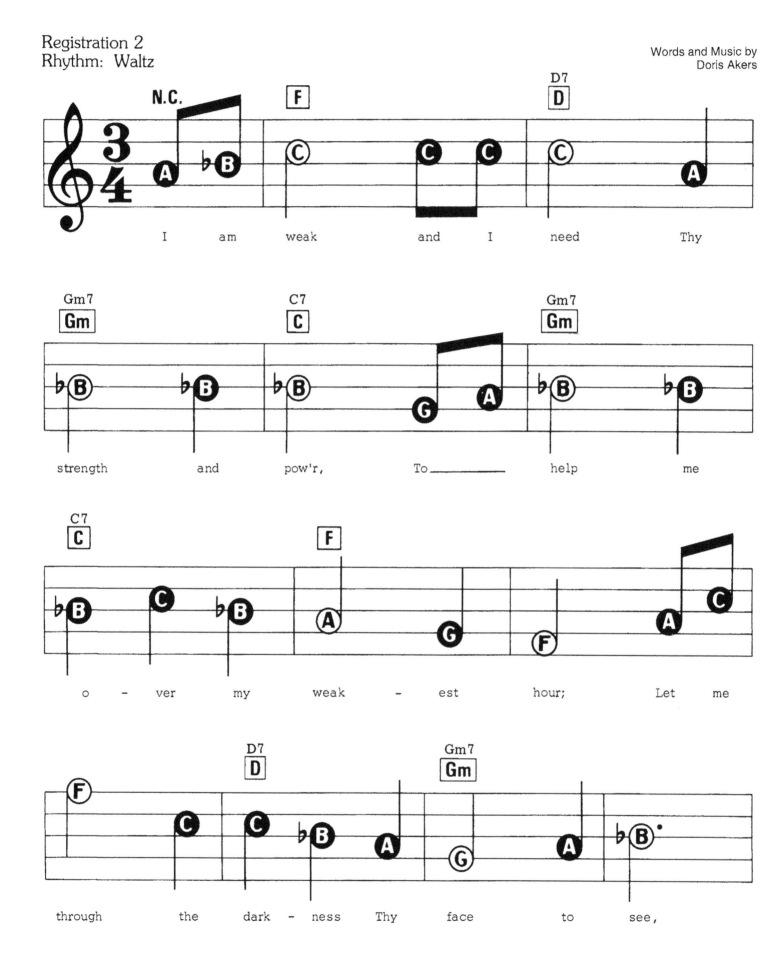

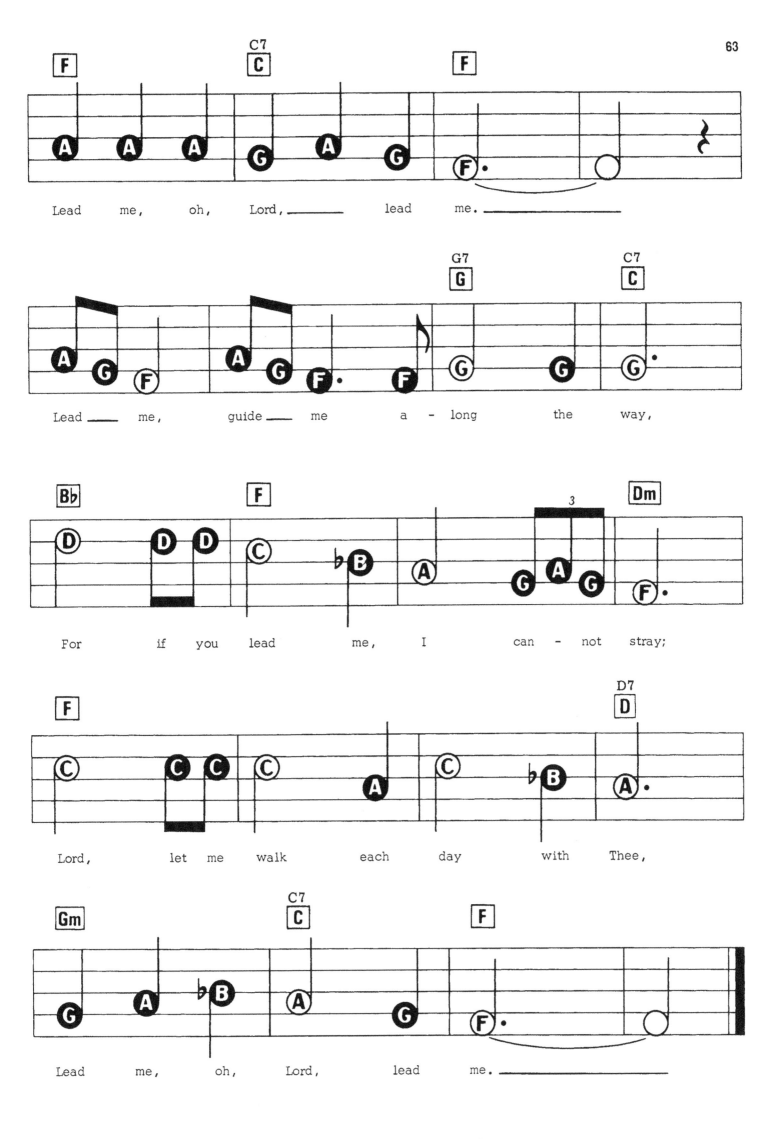

Mansion Over The Hilltop

Registration 5
Rhythm: Swing

Words and Music by
Ira F. Stanphill

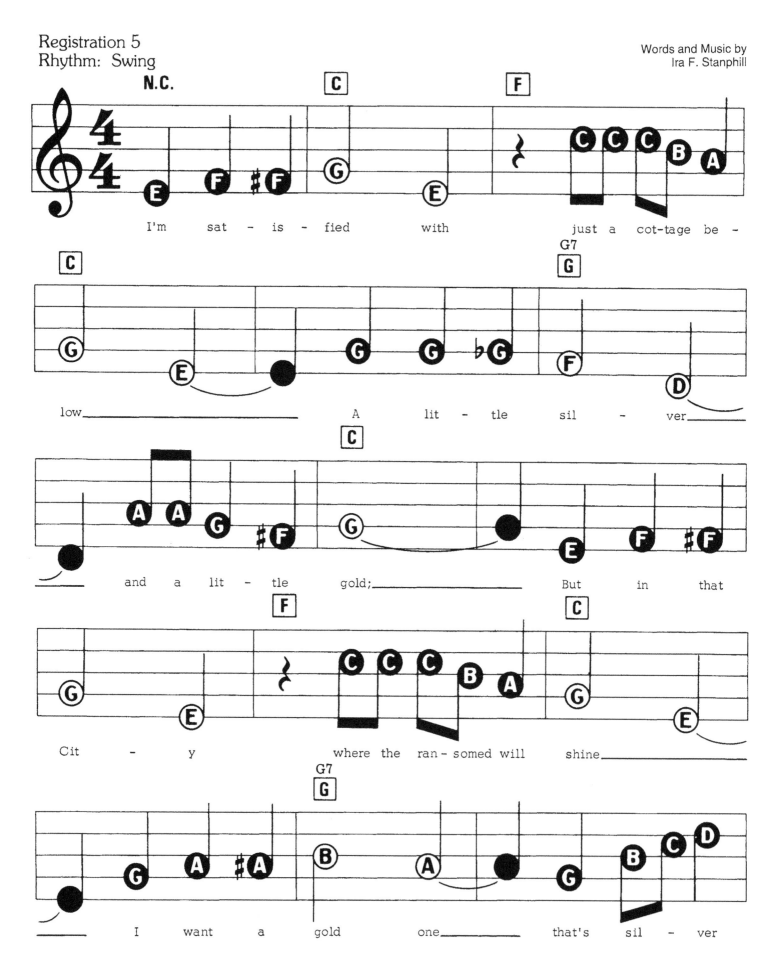

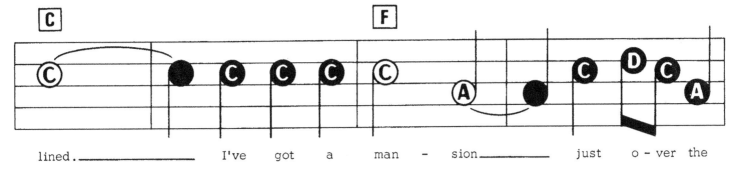

lined._____ I've got a man - sion_____ just o - ver the

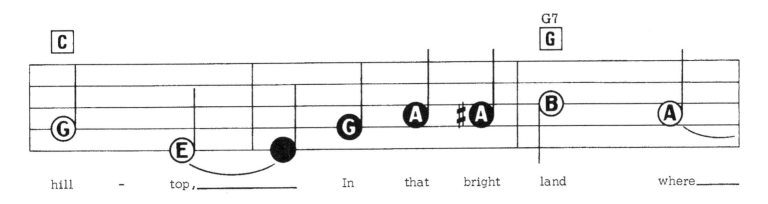

hill - top,_____ In that bright land where_____

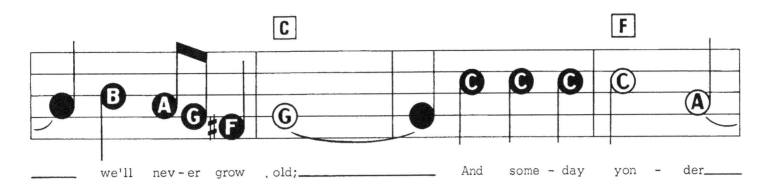

____ we'll nev - er grow old;_____ And some - day yon - der____

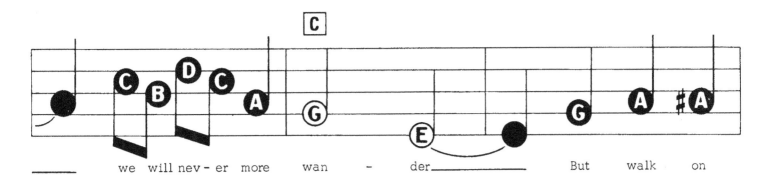

____ we will nev - er more wan - der_____ But walk on

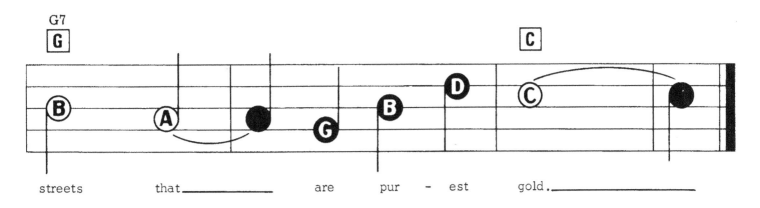

streets that_____ are pur - est gold._____

(There'll Be)
Peace In The Valley
(For Me)

Registration 2
Rhythm: Waltz

Words and Music by
Thomas A. Dorsey

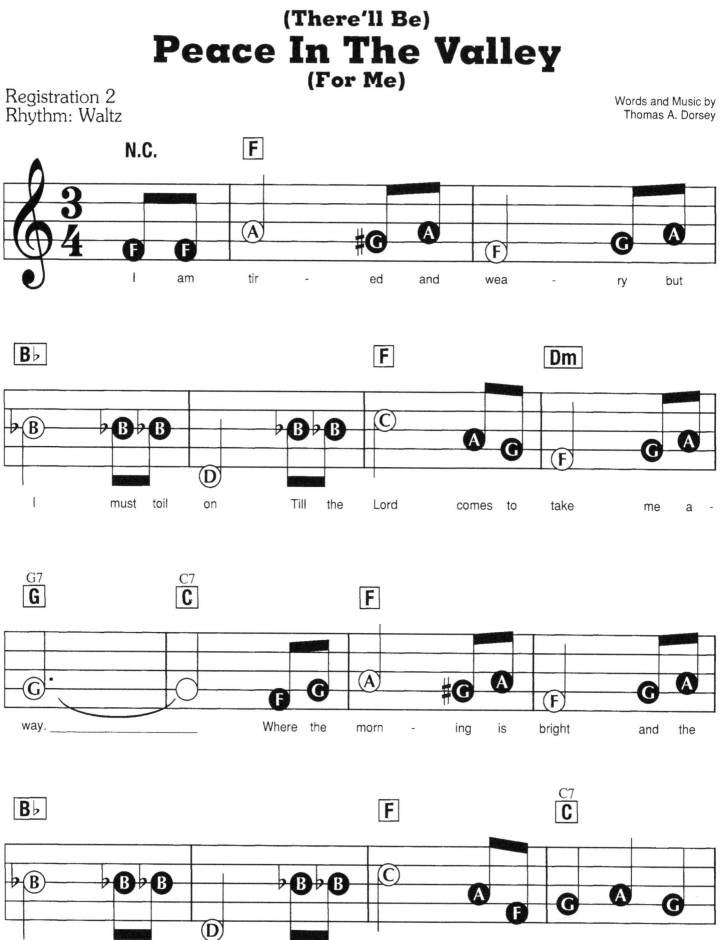

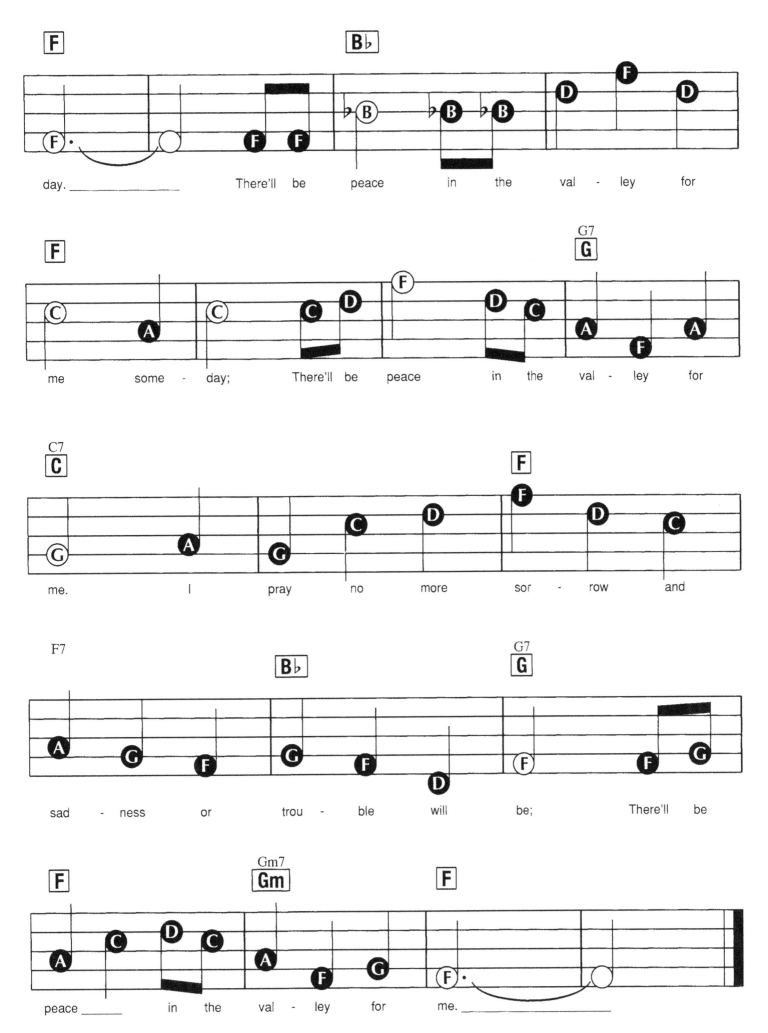

Precious Lord, Take My Hand

(a.k.a. Take My Hand, Precious Lord)

Registration 9
Rhythm: Waltz

Words and Music by
Thomas A. Dorsey

N.C. %: G — G7

3/4

Pre - cious Lord, take my hand, lead me

C — G

on, let me stand, ____ I am tired, ____ I am

D7 / D

weak, I am worn. _____ Thru the

G — G7 — C

storm, thru the night lead me on to the

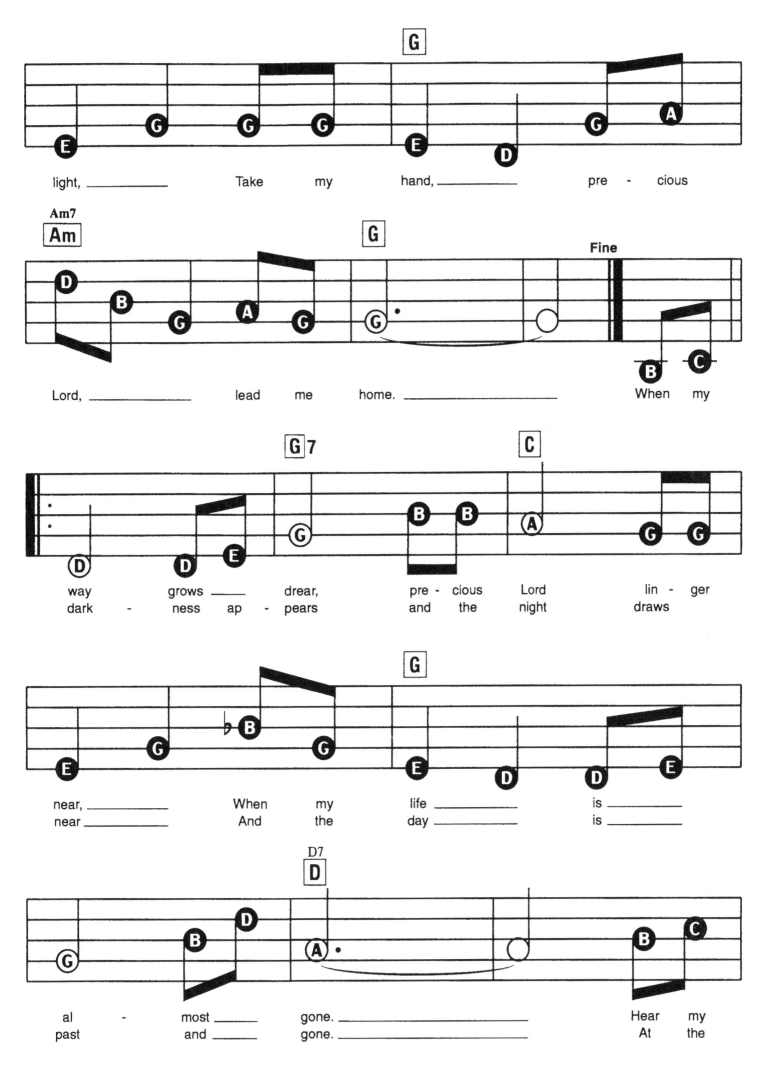

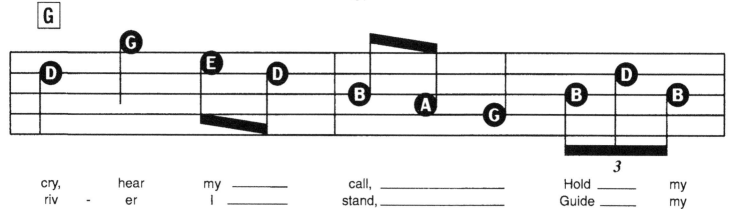

cry,   hear   my _____ call, _____ Hold _____ my
riv - er   I _____ stand, _____ Guide _____ my

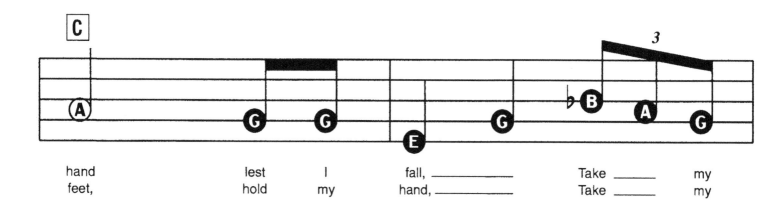

hand,   lest   I   fall, _____ Take _____ my
feet,   hold   my   hand, _____ Take _____ my

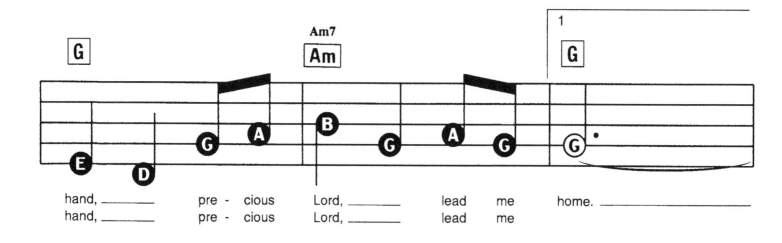

hand, _____ pre - cious Lord, _____ lead me home. _____
hand, _____ pre - cious Lord, _____ lead me

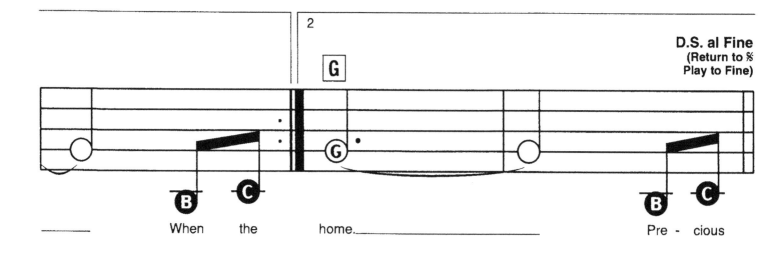

D.S. al Fine
(Return to %
Play to Fine)

_____   When   the   home. _____ Pre - cious

Reach Out To Jesus

Registration 7
Rhythm: Waltz or Jazz Waltz

Words and Music by
Ralph Carmichael

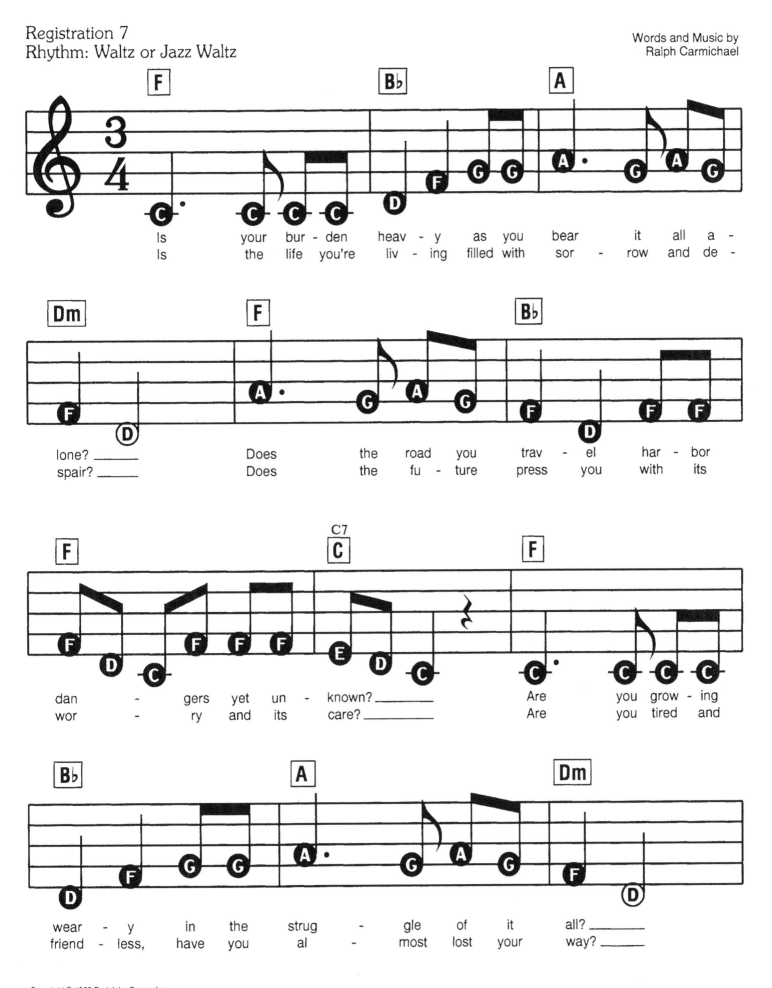

Is your bur - den heav - y as you bear it all a -
Is the life you're liv - ing filled with sor - row and de -

lone? _____ Does the road you trav - el har - bor
spair? _____ Does the fu - ture press you with its

dan - gers yet un - known? _____ Are you grow - ing
wor - ry and its care? _____ Are you tired and

wear - y in the strug - gle of it all? _____
friend - less, have you al - most lost your way? _____

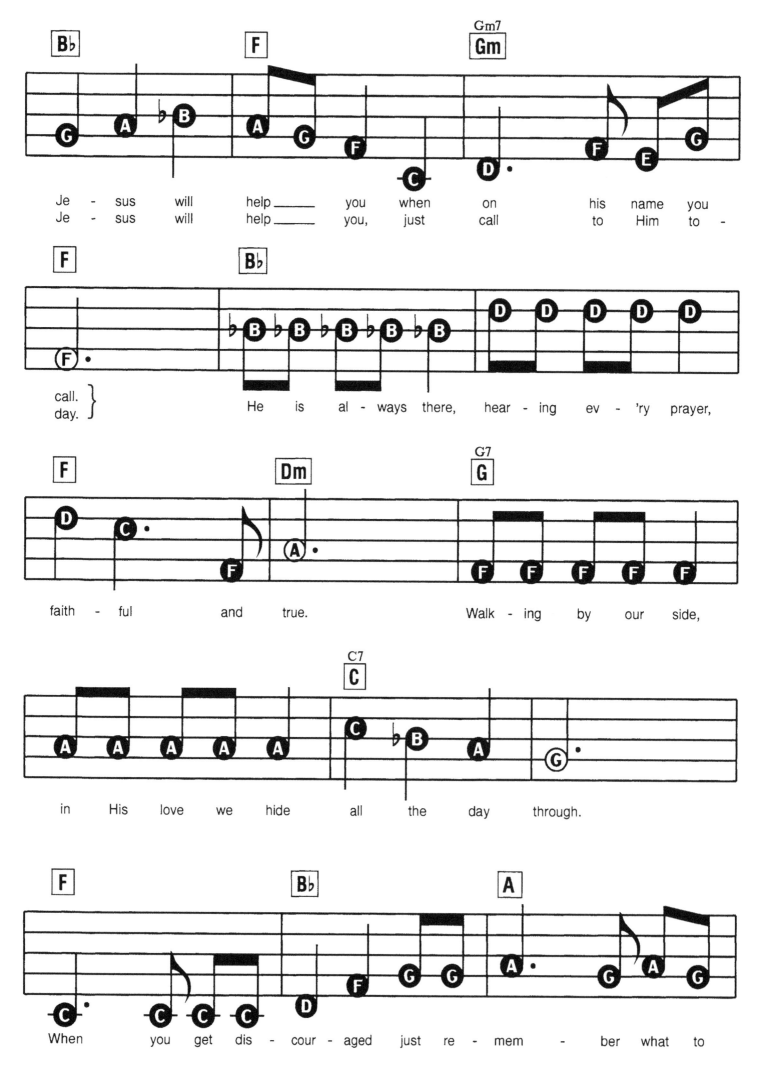

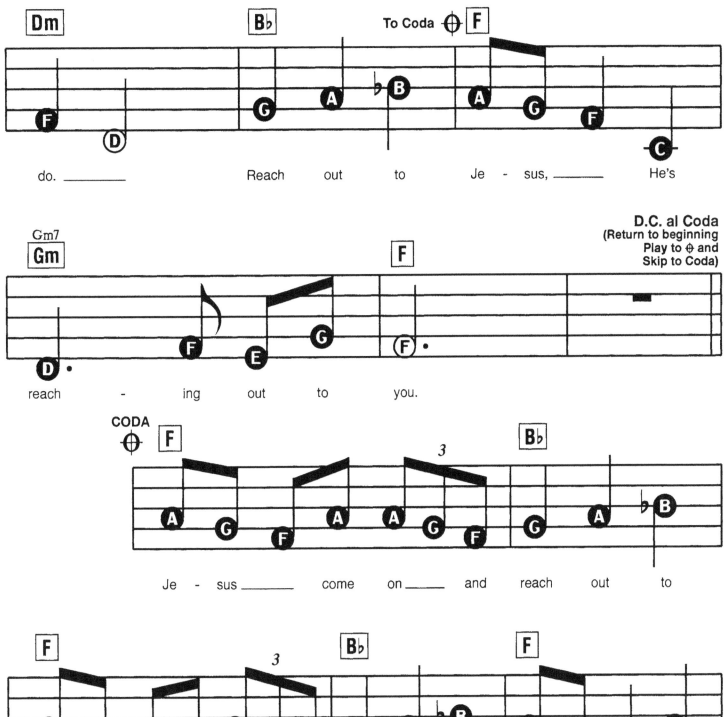

do. _____ Reach out to Je - sus, _____ He's

reach - ing out to you.

D.C. al Coda
(Return to beginning
Play to ⊕ and
Skip to Coda)

CODA

Je - sus _____ come on _____ and reach out to

Je - sus. I said ____ to reach out to Je - sus, He's reach -

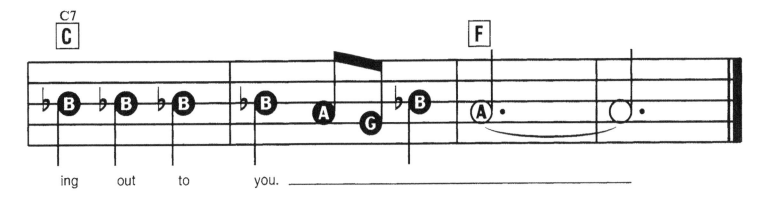

ing out to you. _____

Run On

Registration 9
Rhythm: Shuffle or Swing

Adapted and Arranged by
Elvis Presley

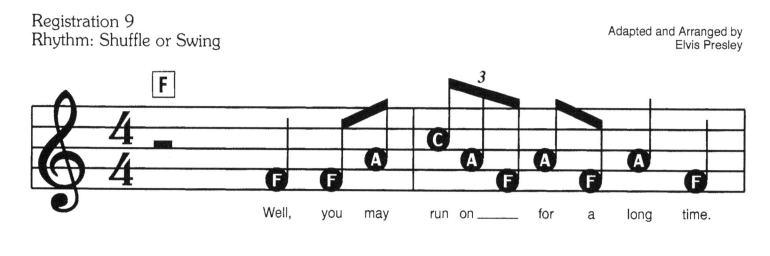

Well, you may run on _____ for a long time.

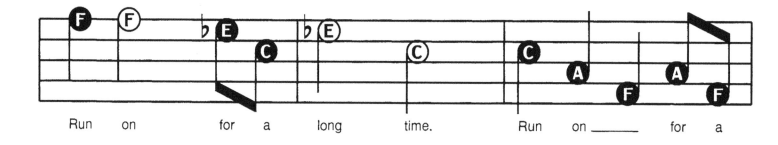

Run on for a long time. Run on _____ for a

long time. Let me tell you God Al - might - y's gon - na

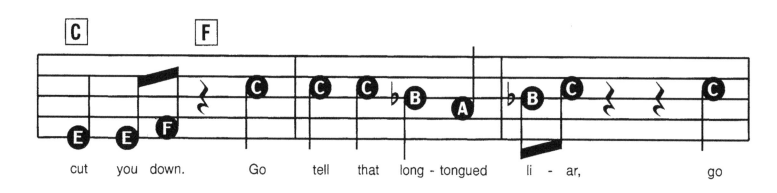

cut you down. Go tell that long - tongued li - ar, go

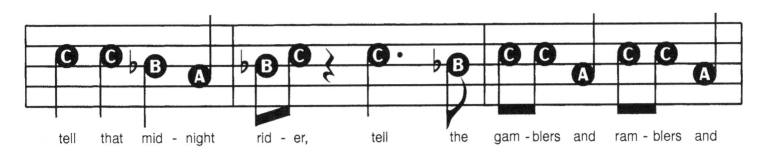

tell that mid - night rid - er, tell the gam - blers and ram - blers and

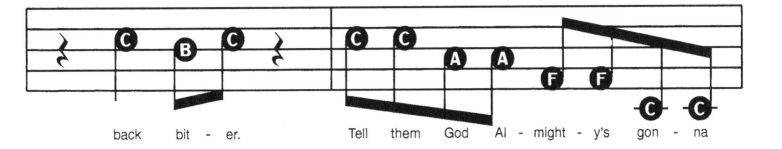

back bit - er. Tell them God Al - might - y's gon - na

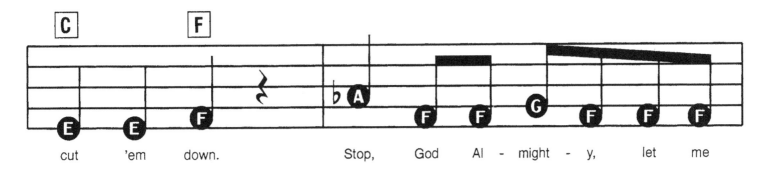

cut 'em down. Stop, God Al - might - y, let me

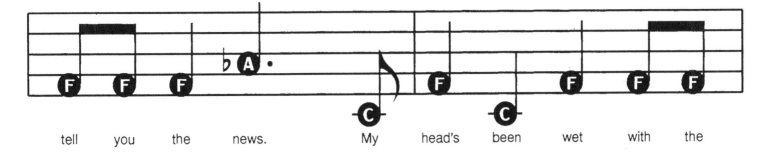

tell you the news. My head's been wet with the

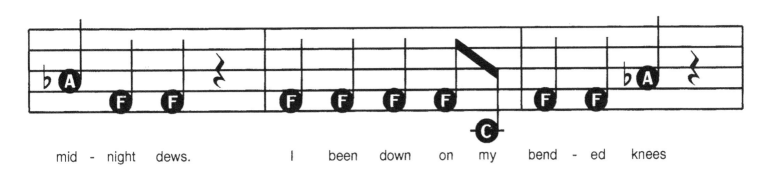

mid - night dews. I been down on my bend - ed knees

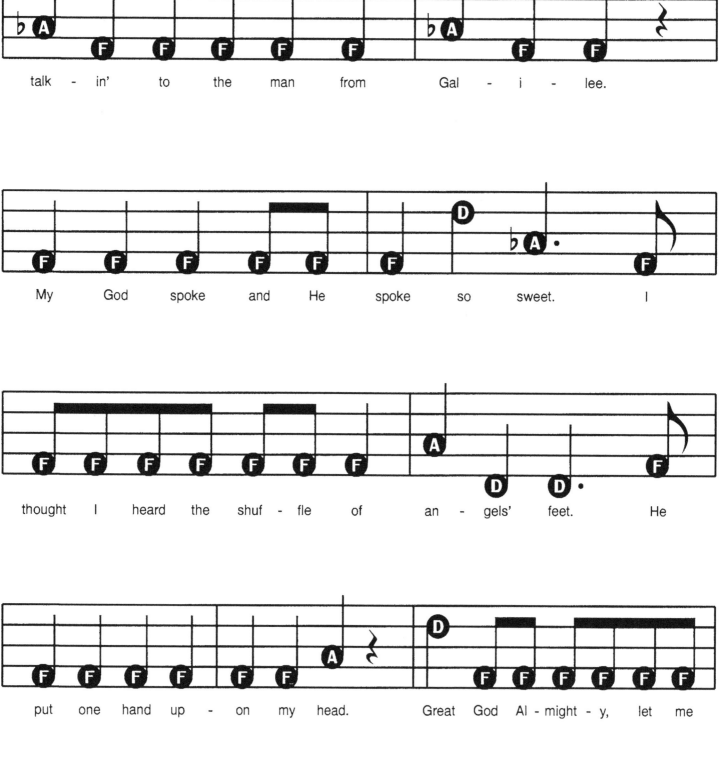

talk - in' to the man from Gal - i - lee.

My God spoke and He spoke so sweet. I

thought I heard the shuf - fle of an - gels' feet. He

put one hand up - on my head. Great God Al - might - y, let me

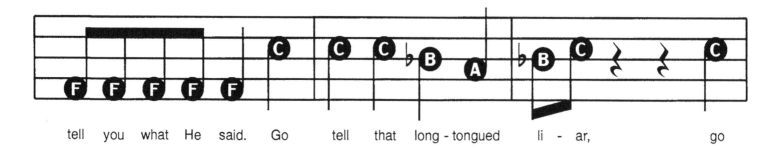

tell you what He said. Go tell that long - tongued li - ar, go

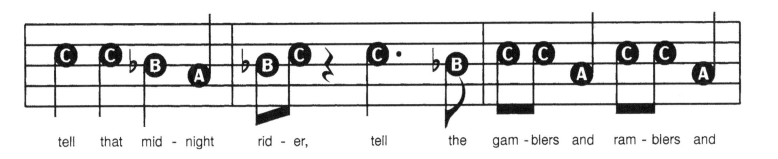

tell that mid - night rid - er, tell the gam -blers and ram - blers and

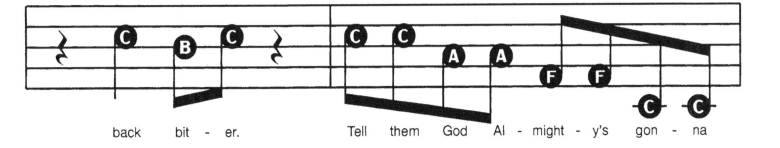

back bit - er. Tell them God Al - might - y's gon - na

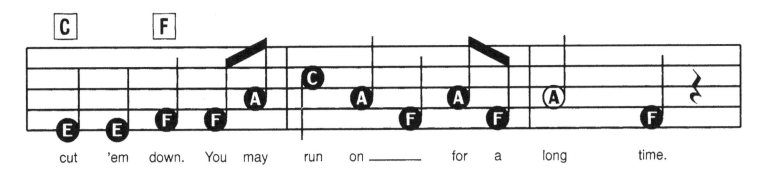

cut 'em down. You may run on _____ for a long time.

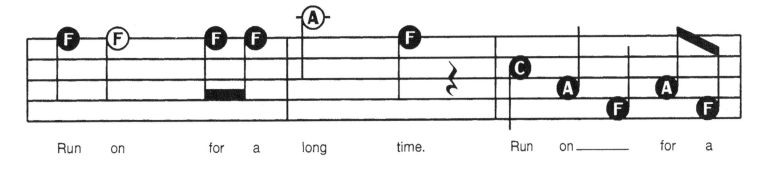

Run on for a long time. Run on _____ for a

long time. Let me tell you God Al - might - y's gon - na

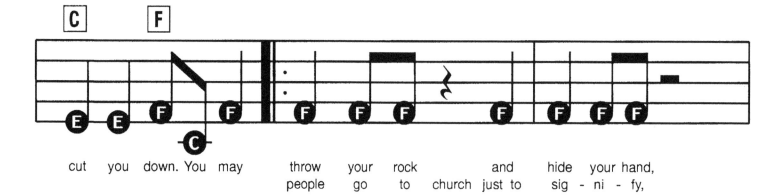

cut you down. You may throw your rock and hide your hand,
people go to church just to sig - ni - fy,

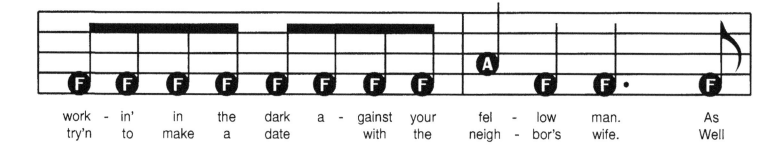

work - in' in the dark a - gainst your fel - low man. As
try'n to make a date with the neigh - bor's wife. Well

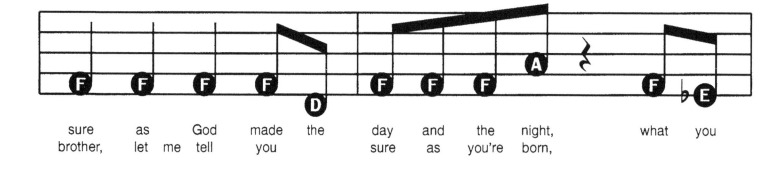

sure as God made the day and the night, what you
brother, let me tell you sure as you're born,

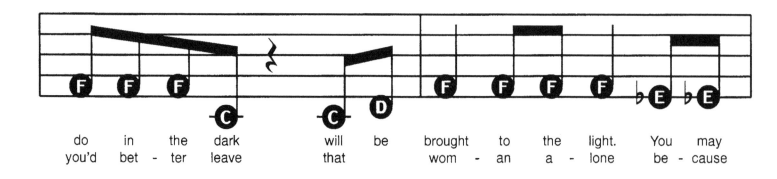

do in the dark will be brought to the light. You may
you'd bet - ter leave that wom - an a - lone be - cause

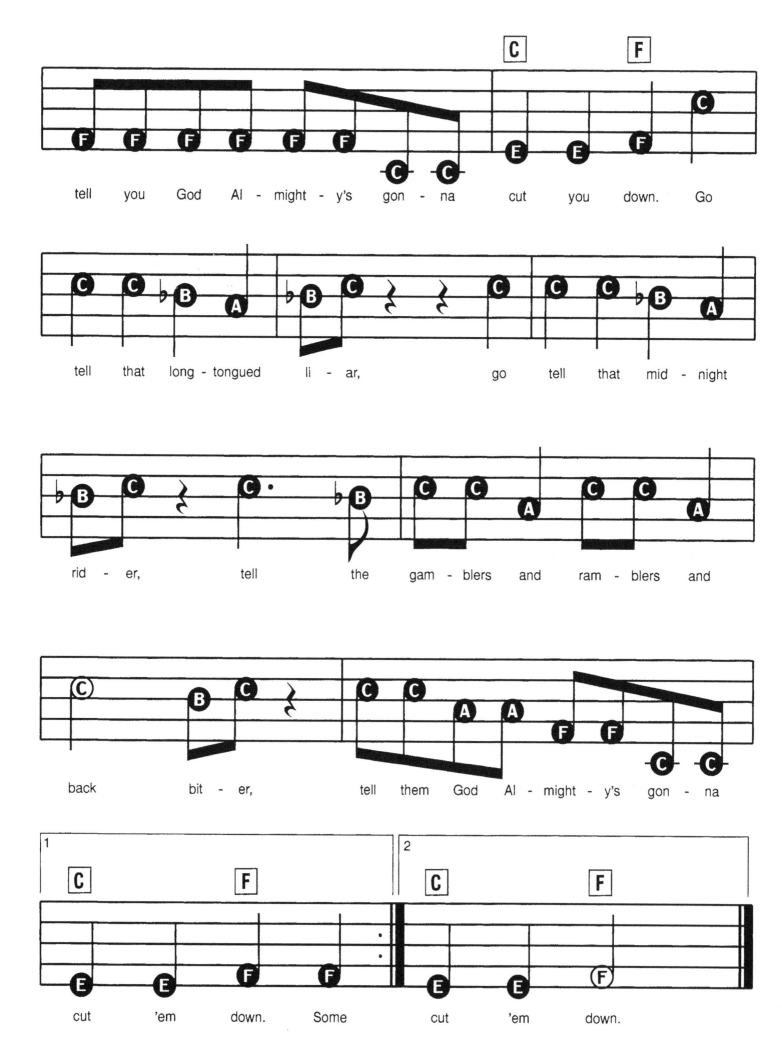

So High

Registration 7
Rhythm: March

Adapted and Arranged by
Elvis Presley

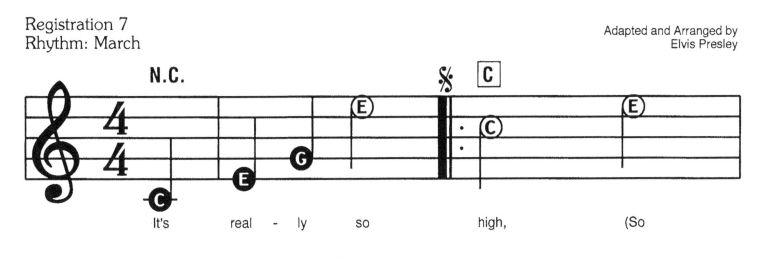

It's real - ly so high, (So

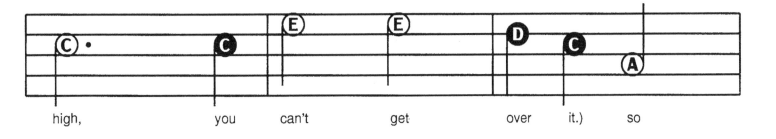

high, you can't get over it.) so

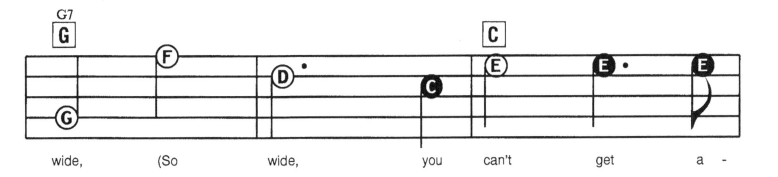

wide, (So wide, you can't get a -

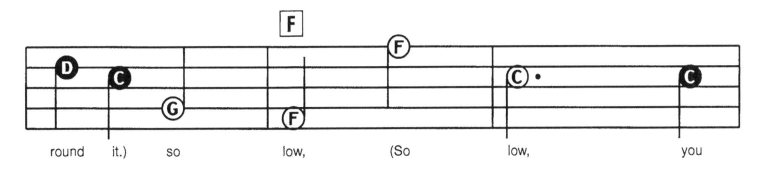

round it.) so low, (So low, you

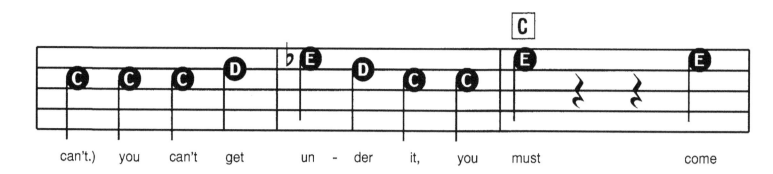

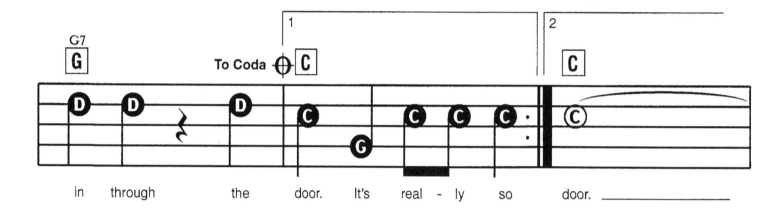

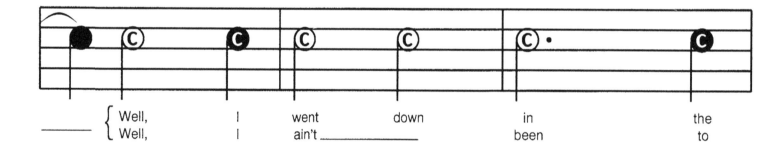

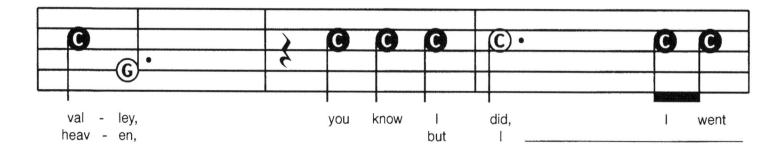

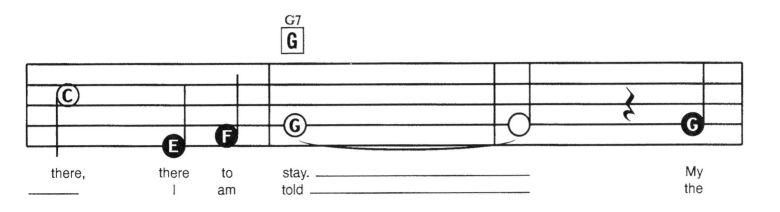

there, | there | to | stay. _____ | My
_____ | I | am | told _____ | the

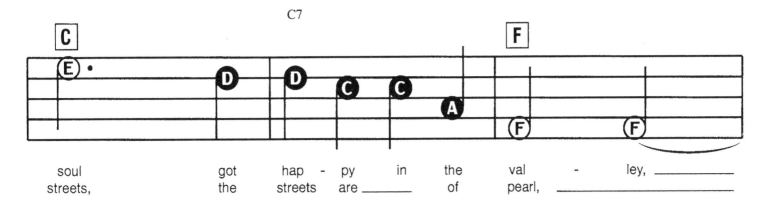

soul | got | hap - py | in | the | val - | ley, _____
streets, | the | streets are ____ | of | pearl, _____

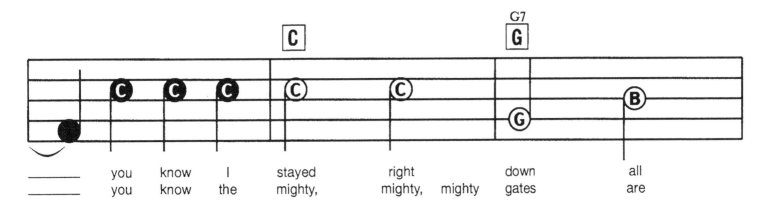

_____ | you know | I | stayed | right | down | all
_____ | you know | the | mighty, | mighty, mighty | gates | are

D.S. al Coda
(Return to 𝄌
Play to 🛇 and
Skip to Coda)

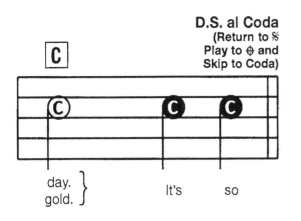

day. ⎫
gold. ⎭ | It's | so

CODA

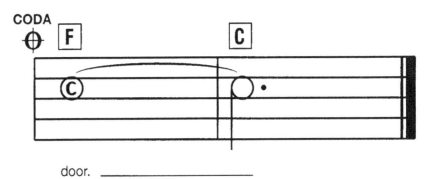

door. _____

Stand By Me

Registration 7
Rhythm: 8-Beat or Rock

Adapted and Arranged by
Elvis Presley

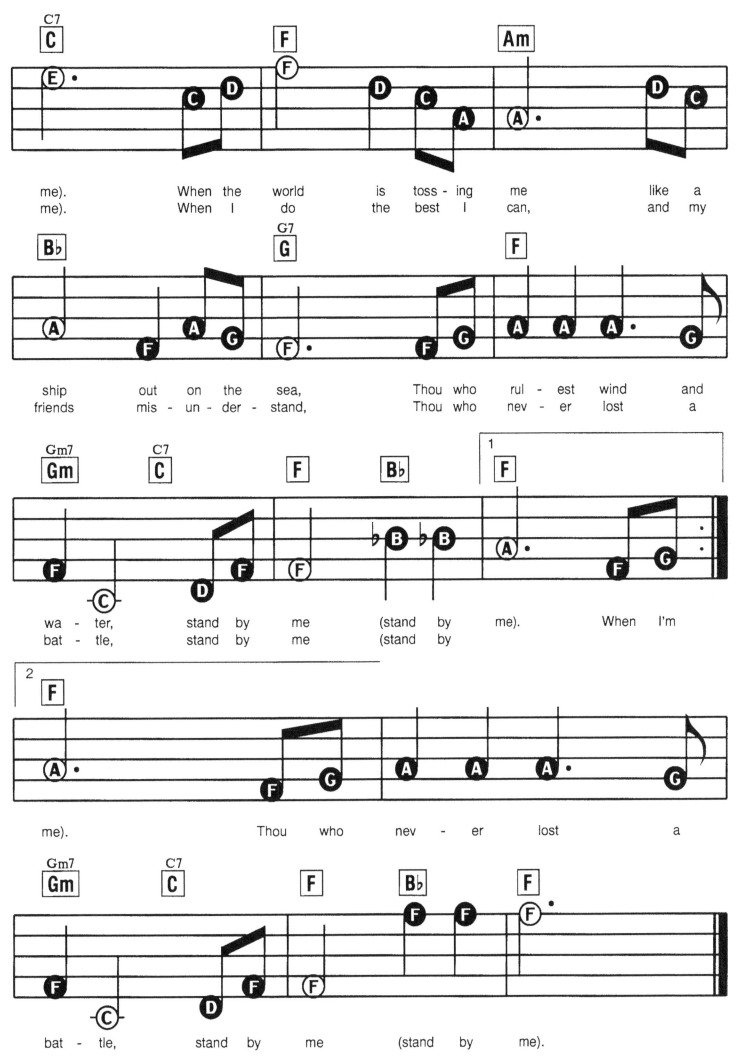

Swing Down, Sweet Chariot

Registration 4
Rhythm: March or Rock

Adapted and Arranged by
Elvis Presley

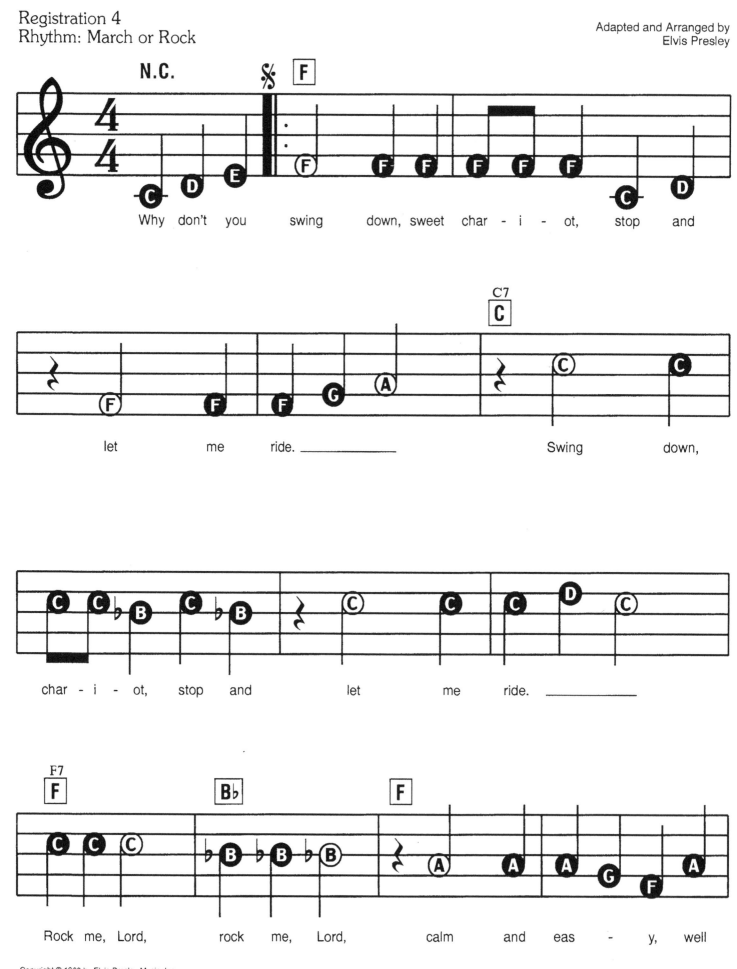

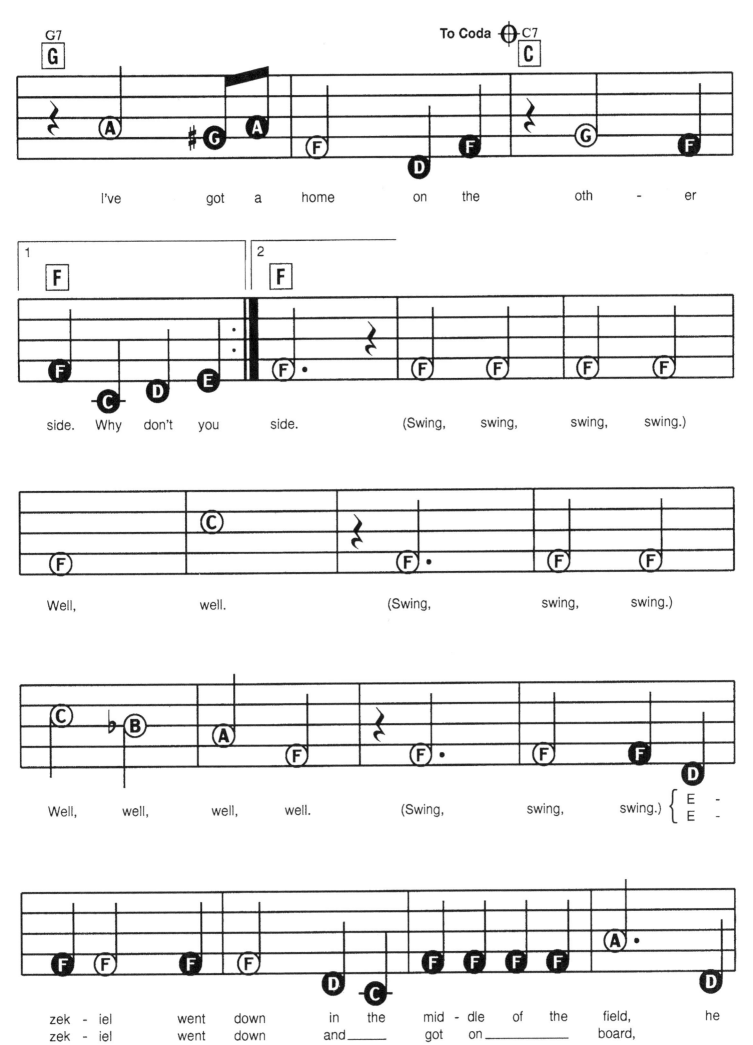

88

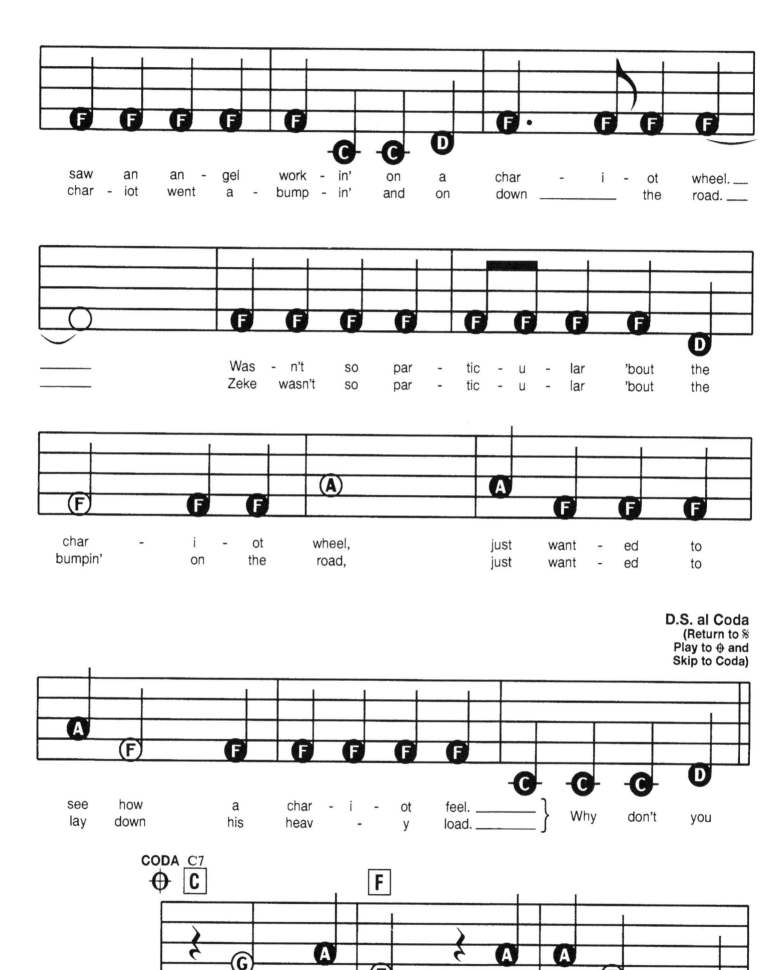

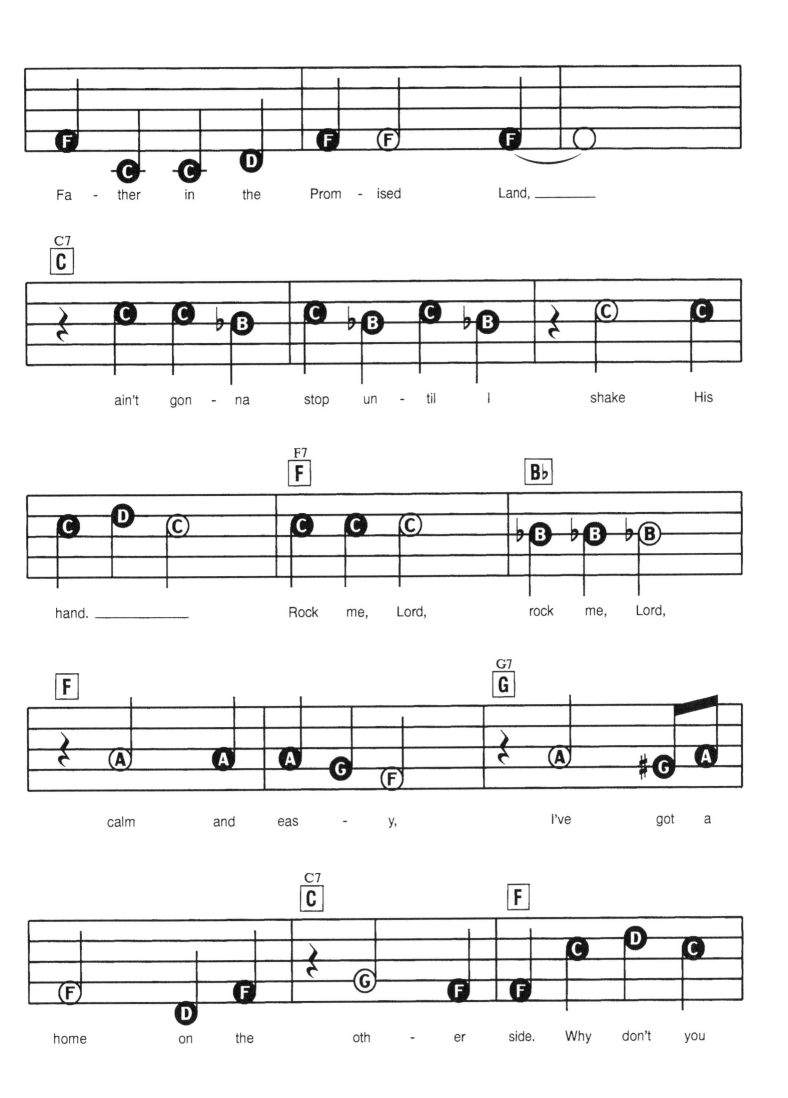

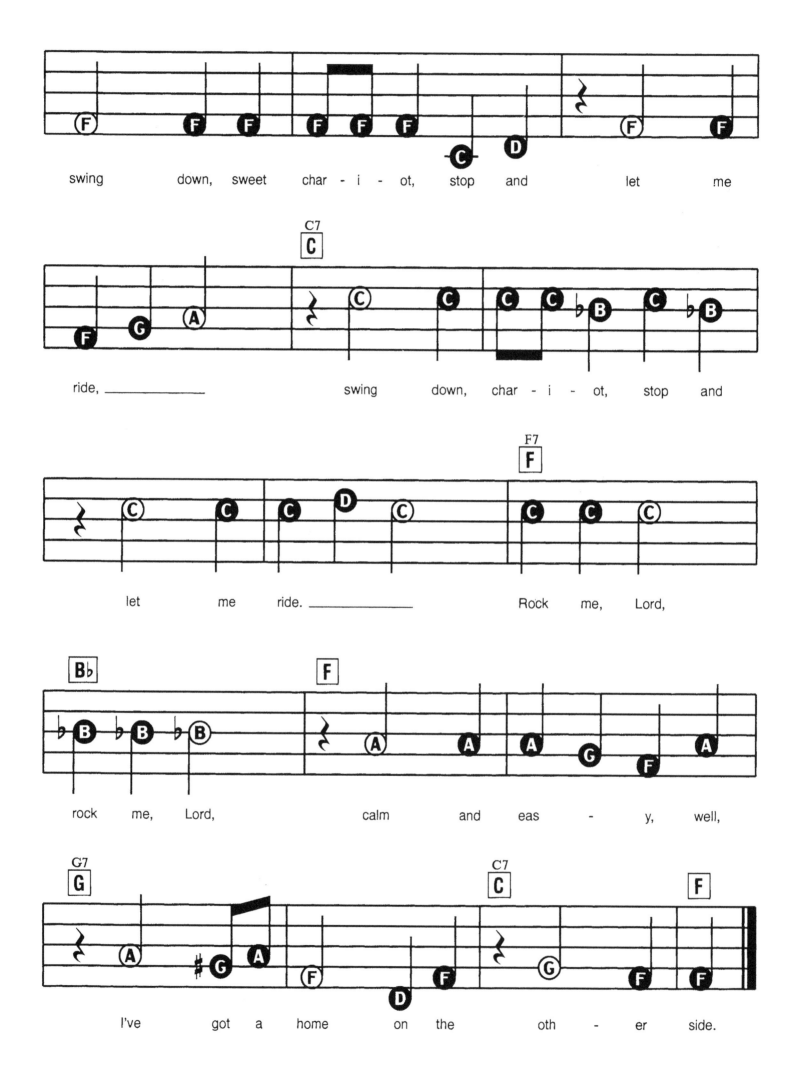

Who Am I

Registration 3
Rhythm: 8 Beat or Pops

By Rusty Goodman

place,   then I ask   my - self   the   ques - tion, "Who am
Son,   fight my bat - tles   'til   they're   won, _____ who am

I?" _____ }
I? _____ }   Who   am   I   that   a

king   would   bleed   and   die   for? _____   Who   am

I   that   He   would   pray,   "Not   my   will,

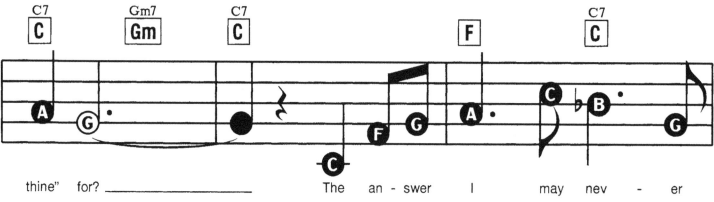

thine" for? _____   The   an - swer   I   may   nev - er

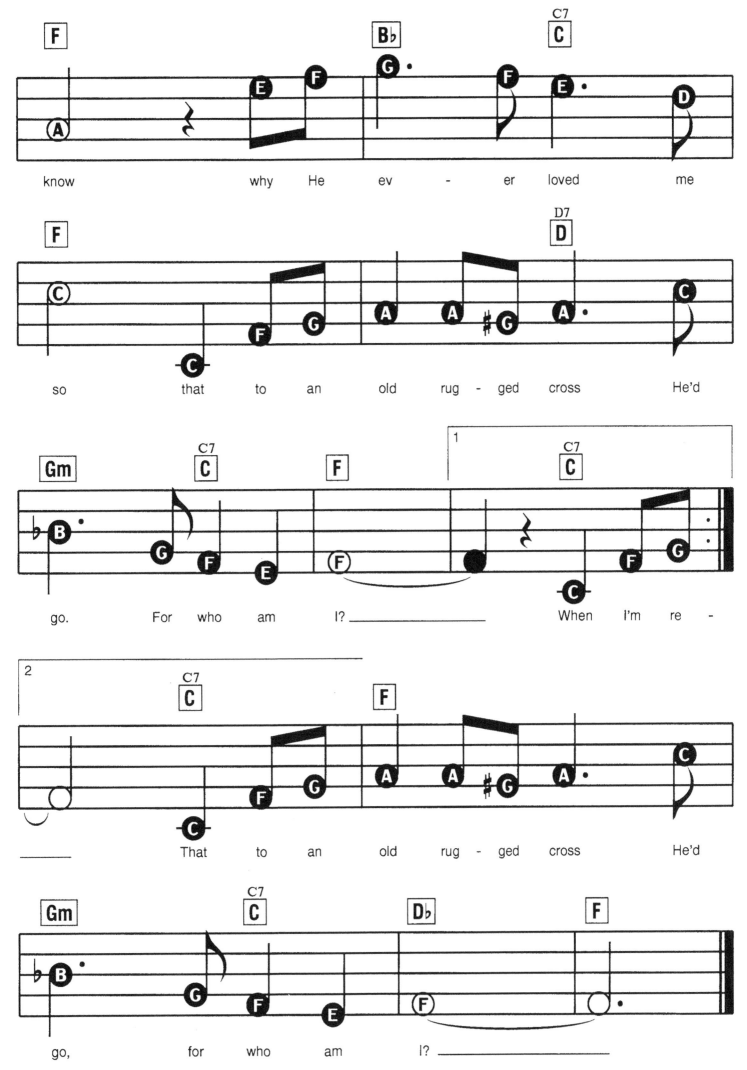

Up Above My Head

Registration 8
Rhythm: Pops or Rock

Adapted and Arranged by
W. Earl Brown

Up a - bove my head

there is mu - sic in the air.

Up a - bove my head

there is mu - sic in the air.

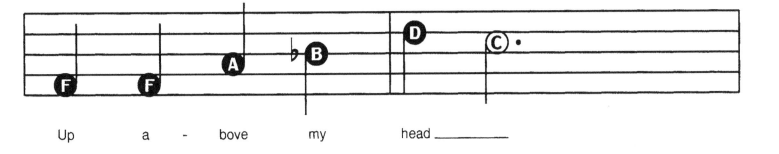

Up a - bove my head _____

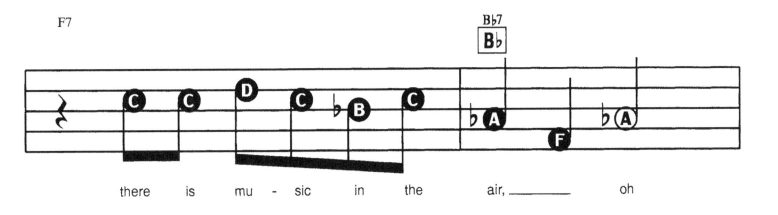

there is mu - sic in the air, _____ oh

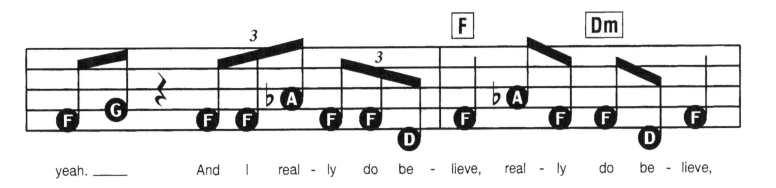

yeah. ____ And I real - ly do be - lieve, real - ly do be - lieve,

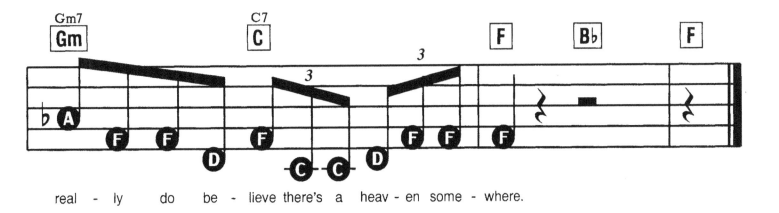

real - ly do be - lieve there's a heav - en some - where.

We Call On Him

Registration 10
Rhythm: 8 Beat or Pops

Words and Music by Ben Weisman,
Sid Wayne and Fred Karger

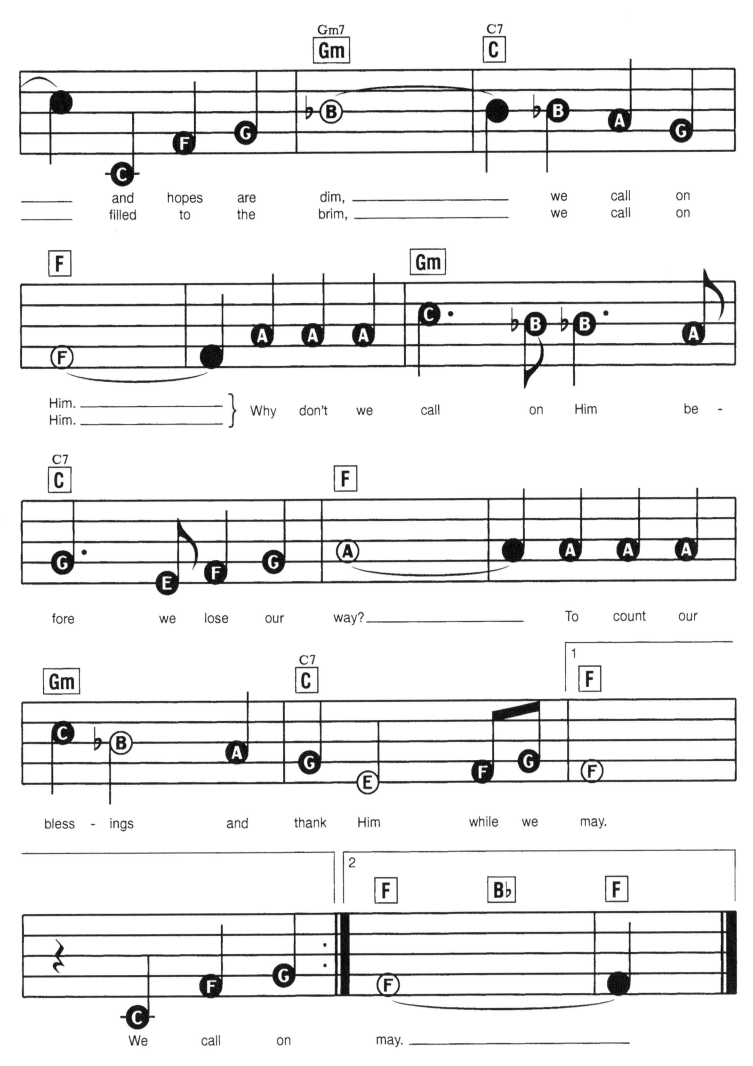

Where Could I Go

Registration 8
Rhythm: Pops or 8 Beat

Words and Music by
James B. Coats

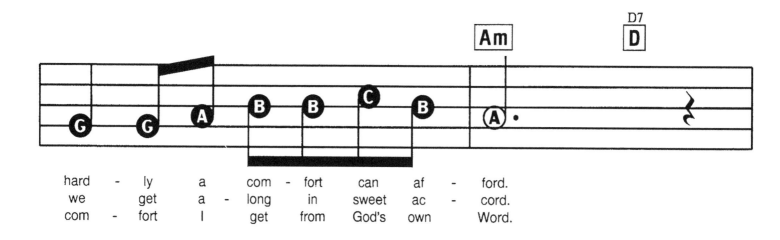

Liv - ing be - low   in   this old sin - ful world,
Neigh - bors are kind,   I   love them ev - 'ry one,
Life here is grand   with friends I love so dear,

hard - ly   a com - fort can af - ford.
we   get   a - long in sweet ac - cord.
com - fort I   get from God's own Word.

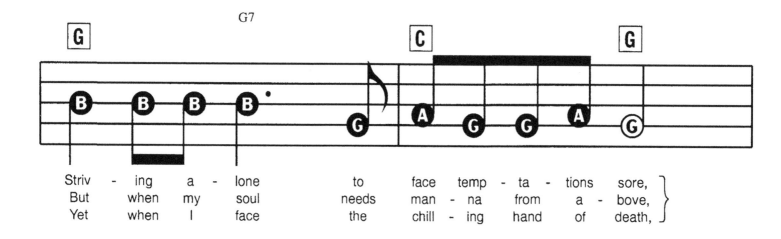

Striv - ing a - lone   to   face temp - ta - tions sore,
But when my soul   needs man - na from a - bove,
Yet when I face   the chill - ing hand of death,

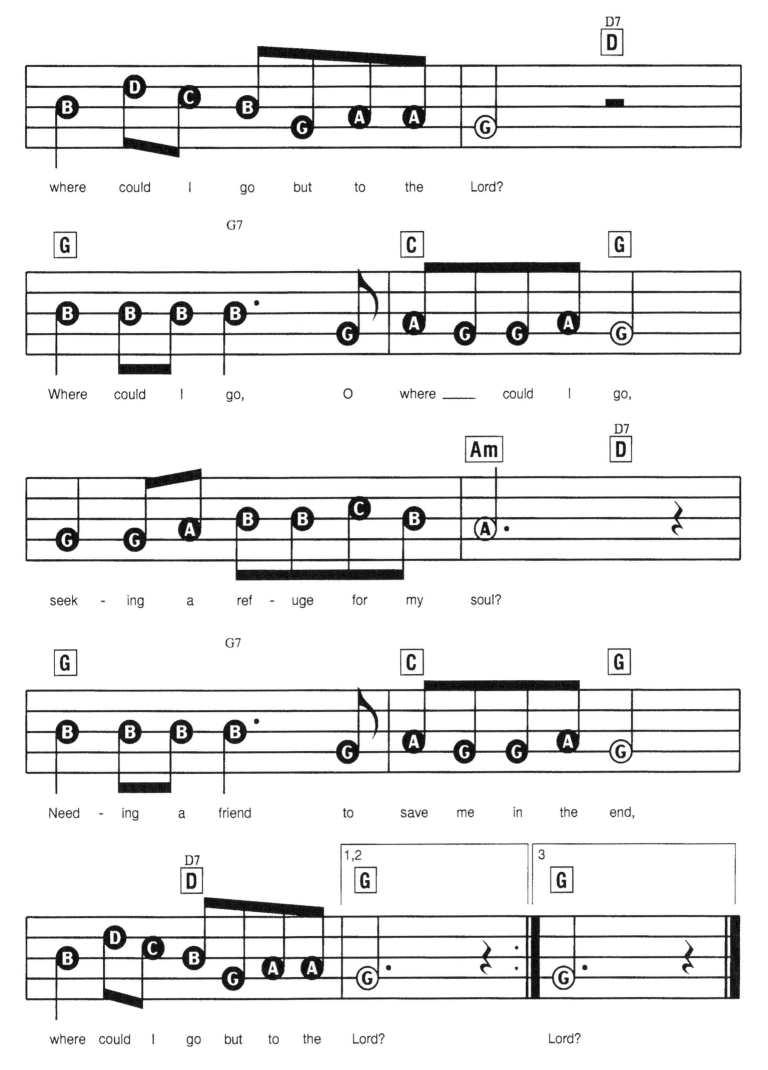

Working On The Building

Registration 7
Rhythm: Swing or Bounce

Words and Music by W.O. Hoyle
and Lillian Bowles

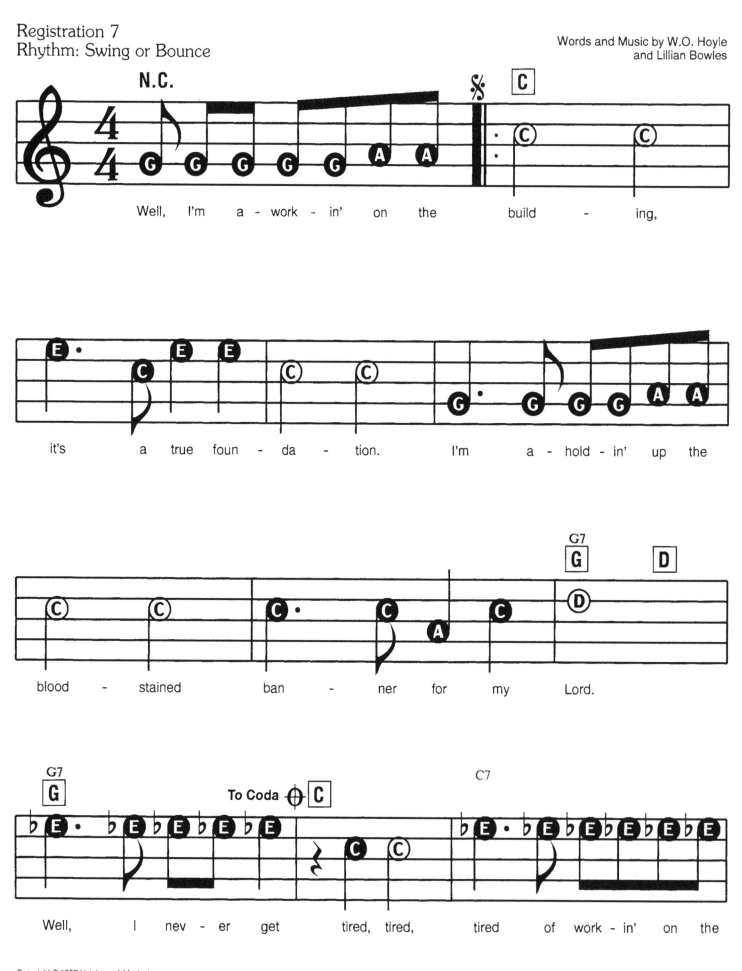

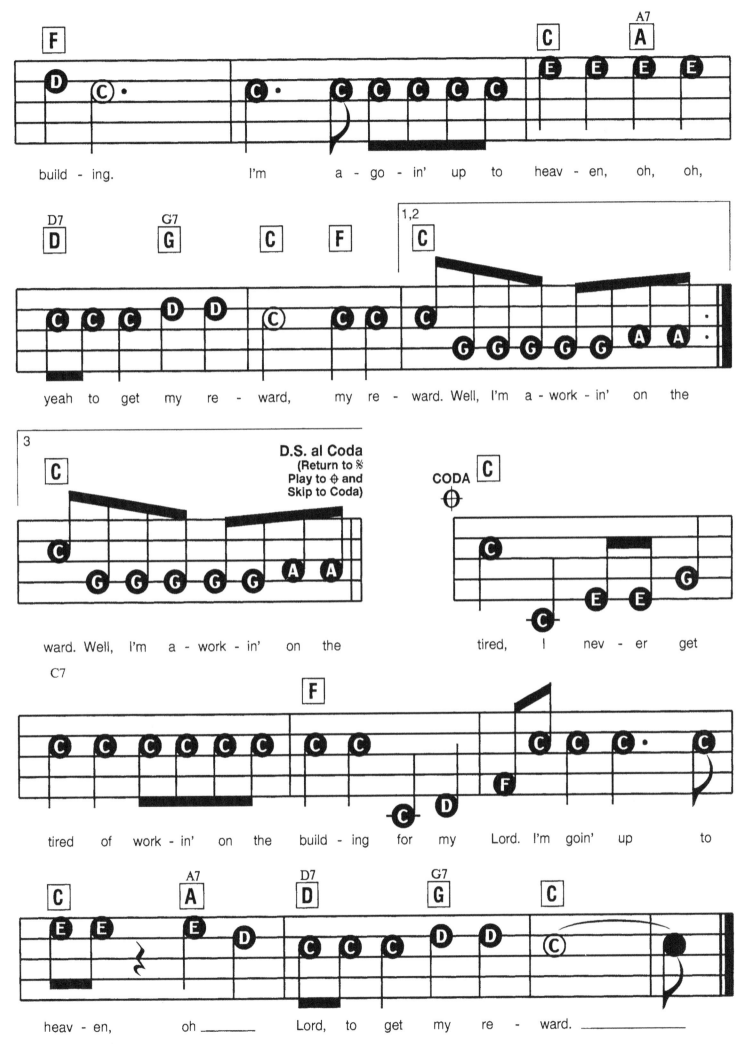

You'll Never Walk Alone
(From "CAROUSEL")

Registration 5
Rhythm: Ballad

Lyrics by Oscar Hammerstein II
Music by Richard Rodgers

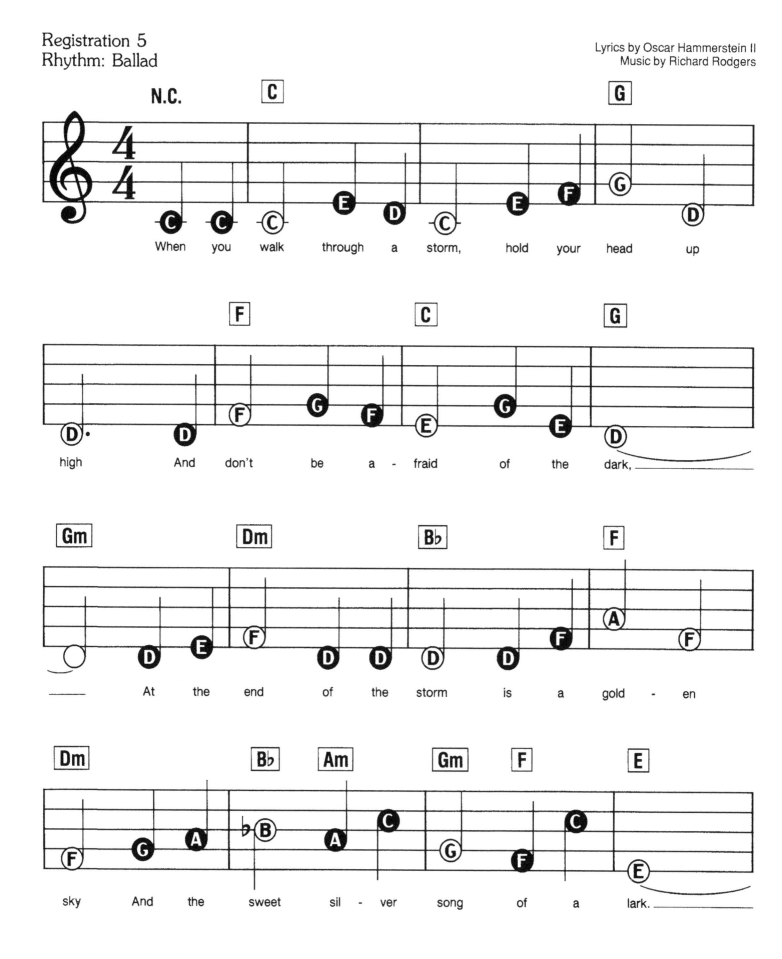

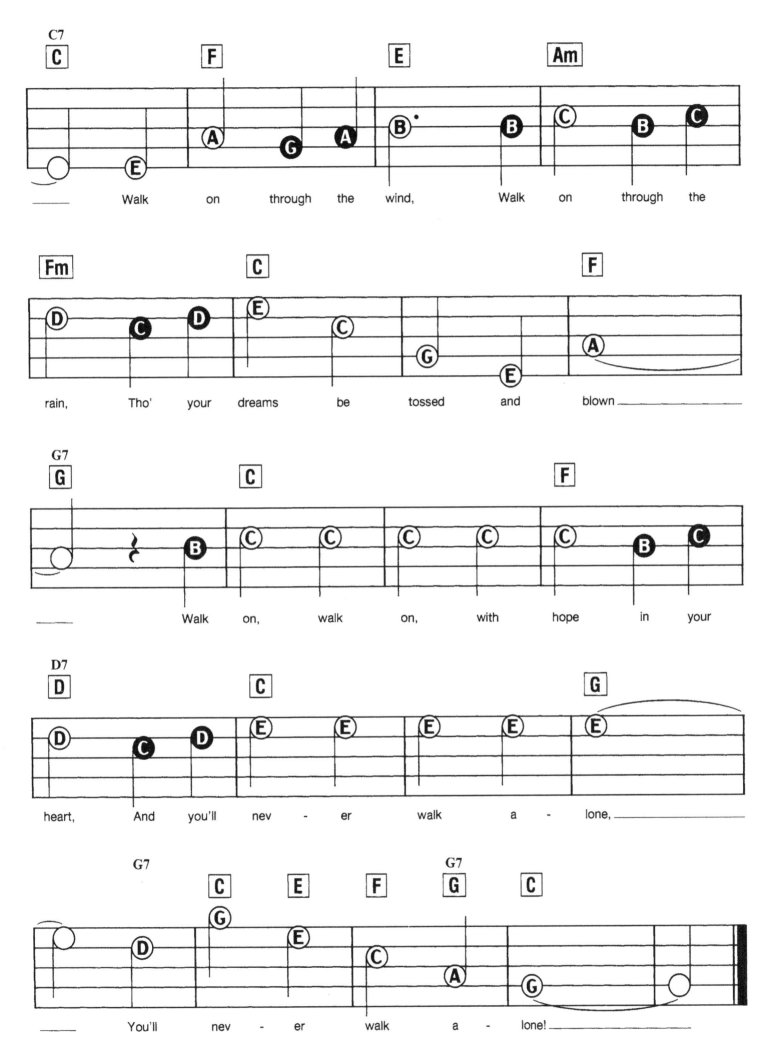

Registration Guide

- Match the Registration number on the song to the corresponding numbered category below. Select and activate an instrumental sound available on your instrument.

- Choose an automatic rhythm appropriate to the mood and style of the song. (Consult your Owner's Guide for proper operation of automatic rhythm features.)

- Adjust the tempo and volume controls to comfortable settings.

Registration

1	Flute, Pan Flute, Jazz Flute
2	Clarinet, Organ
3	Violin, Strings
4	Brass, Trumpet, Bass
5	Synth Ensemble, Accordion, Brass
6	Pipe Organ, Harpsichord
7	Jazz Organ, Vibraphone, Vibes, Electric Piano, Jazz Guitar
8	Piano, Electric Piano
9	Trumpet, Trombone, Clarinet, Saxophone, Oboe
10	Violin, Cello, Strings